BUILDING VOCABULARY SKILLS

SHORT VERSION / Third Edition

BUILDING VOCABULARY SKILLS

SHORT VERSION / Third Edition

SHERRIE L. NIST
UNIVERSITY OF GEORGIA

CAROLE MOHR

TOWNSEND PRESS

Books in the Townsend Press Vocabulary Series:

Vocabulary Basics
Groundwork for a Better Vocabulary
Building Vocabulary Skills
Building Vocabulary Skills, Short Version
Improving Vocabulary Skills
Improving Vocabulary Skills, Short Version
Advancing Vocabulary Skills
Advancing Vocabulary Skills, Short Version
Advanced Word Power

Books in the Townsend Press Reading Series:

Groundwork for College Reading
Groundwork for College Reading with Phonics
Ten Steps to Building College Reading Skills
Ten Steps to Improving College Reading Skills
Ten Steps to Advancing College Reading Skills
Ten Steps to Advanced Reading

Other Reading and Writing Books:

Everyday Heroes
Voices and Values: A Reader for Writers
English at Hand
English Essentials

Supplements Available for Most Books:

Instructor's Edition
Instructor's Manual and Test Bank
Online Exercises

Copyright © 2002 by Townsend Press, Inc.
Printed in the United States of America
9 8 7 6 5 4

ISBN-13: 978-0-944210-15-4
ISBN-10: 0-944210-15-5

Send book orders and requests for desk copies or supplements to:
Townsend Press Book Center
439 Kelley Drive
West Berlin, New Jersey 08091

For even faster service, contact us in any of the following ways:
By telephone: 1-800-772-6410
By fax: 1-800-225-8894
By e-mail: cs@townsendpress.com
Through our website: www.townsendpress.com

Contents

Note: For ease of reference, the title of the selection that closes each chapter is included.

Preface

The problem is all too familiar: *students just don't know enough words*. Reading, writing, and content teachers agree that many students' vocabularies are inadequate for the demands of courses. Weak vocabularies limit students' understanding of what they read and the clarity and depth of what they write.

The purpose of the Townsend Press vocabulary series is to provide a solid, workable answer to the vocabulary problem. The short version of the series consists of three books, each of which teaches 200 important words. Within each book are twenty chapters, with ten words in each chapter. Here are the distinctive features of *Building Vocabulary Skills, Short Version, Third Edition:*

1 **An intensive words-in-context approach.** Studies show that students learn words best by reading them repeatedly in different contexts, not through rote memorization. The book gives students an intensive in-context experience by presenting each word in six different contexts. Each chapter takes students through a productive sequence of steps:

- Students infer the meaning of each word by considering two sentences in which it appears and then choosing from multiple-choice options.
- On the basis of their inferences, students identify each word's meaning in a matching test. They are then in a solid position to deepen their knowledge of a word.
- Finally, they strengthen their understanding of a word by applying it three times: in two sentence practices and in a selection practice.

Each encounter with a word brings it closer to becoming part of the student's permanent word bank.

2 **Abundant practice.** Along with extensive practice in each chapter, there are a crossword puzzle and a set of unit tests at the end of every five-chapter unit. The puzzle and tests reinforce students' knowledge of the words in each chapter. In addition, most chapters reuse several words from earlier chapters (such repeated words are marked with small circles), allowing for more reinforcement. Last, there are supplementary tests in the *Test Bank* and the computer software that accompany the book. All this practice means that students learn in the surest possible way: by working closely and repeatedly with each word.

3 **Controlled feedback.** The opening activity in each chapter gives students three multiple-choice options to help them decide on the meaning of a given word. The multiple-choice options also help students to complete the matching test that is the second activity of each chapter. A limited answer key at the back of the book then provides answers for the third activity in the chapter. All these features enable students to take an active role in their own learning.

4 Focus on essential words. A good deal of time and research went into selecting the 200 words featured in the book. Word frequency lists were consulted, along with lists in a wide range of vocabulary books. In addition, the authors and editors each prepared their own lists. A computer was used to help in the consolidation of the many word lists. A long process of group discussion then led to final decisions about the words that would be most helpful for students on a basic reading level.

5 Appealing content. Dull practice materials work against learning. On the other hand, meaningful, lively, and at times even funny sentences and selections can spark students' attention and thus enhance their grasp of the material. For this reason, a great deal of effort was put into creating sentences and selections with both widespread appeal and solid context support. We have tried throughout to make the practice materials truly enjoyable for teachers and students alike. Look, for example, at the selection on page 11 that closes the first chapter of this book.

6 Clear format. The book has been designed so that its very format contributes to the learning process. Each chapter consists of two two-page spreads. In the first two-page spread (the first such spread is on pages 8–9), students can easily refer to all ten words in context while working on the matching test, which provides a clear meaning for each word. In the second two-page spread, students can refer to a box that shows all ten words while they work through the fill-in activities on these pages.

7 Supplementary materials.

a A convenient *Instructor's Edition* is available at no charge to instructors using the book. It is identical to the student book except that it contains answers to all of the activities and tests.

b A combined *Instructor's Manual and Test Bank* is also offered at no charge to instructors who have adopted the book. This booklet contains a general vocabulary placement test as well as a pretest and a posttest for the book and for each of the four units in the text. It also includes teaching guidelines, suggested syllabi, an answer key, and an additional mastery test for each chapter as well as an additional mastery test for each unit.

c *Interactive computer software* also accompanies the book. Free to adopters of 20 or more copies, this software—in both Windows and Macintosh format—provides two additional tests for each vocabulary chapter in the book. The tests include a number of user- and instructor-friendly features: brief explanations of answers (thus the software teaches as well as tests), a sound option, mouse support, icons, color, dialog balloons, frequent mention of the user's first name, a running score at the bottom of the screen, a record-keeping file, and actual, audible pronunciations of each word. Students can access their scores at any time; instructors can access student scores by selecting Administrator mode and entering the appropriate password.

Probably in no other area of reading instruction is the computer more useful than in reinforcing vocabulary. The Townsend Press vocabulary software takes full advantage of the computer's unique capabilities and motivational appeal. Here's how the program works:

- Students are tested on the ten words in a chapter, with each word in a sentence context different from any in the book itself.

- After students answer each question, they receive immediate feedback: The computer indicates if a student is right or wrong and why, frequently using the student's first name and providing a running score.

- When the test is over, the computer supplies a test score and—this especially is what is unique about this program—a chance to take the test a second time. Students then receive a separate score for the retest. The value of this approach is that the computer gives students immediate added practice in words they need to review.

- In addition, the computer offers a second, more challenging "Definitions" test in which students must identify the meanings of the chapter words without benefit of context. This test is a final check that students have really learned the words. And, again, there is the option of a retest.

By the end of this program, students' knowledge of each word in the chapter will have been carefully reinforced. And this reinforcement will be the more effective for having occurred in an electronic medium that especially engages today's students.

To obtain a copy of any of the above materials, instructors who have adopted the book may write to the Reading Editor, Townsend Press, 1038 Industrial Drive, West Berlin, NJ 08091. Alternatively, instructors may call our toll-free number: 1-800-772-6410; send a fax toll-free to 1-800-225-8894, or e-mail our Customer Service department at <townsendcs@aol.com>.

8 Realistic pricing. As with the previous editions, the goal has been to offer the highest possible quality at the best possible price. While *Building Vocabulary Skills, Short Version* is comprehensive enough to serve as a primary text, its modest price also makes it an inexpensive supplement.

9 One in a sequence of books. The most fundamental book in the Townsend Press vocabulary series is *Vocabulary Basics*. It is followed by *Groundwork for a Better Vocabulary* (a slightly more advanced basic text) and then by the three main books in the series: *Building Vocabulary Skills* (also a basic text), *Improving Vocabulary Skills* (an intermediate text), and *Advancing Vocabulary Skills* (a more advanced text). The most advanced book in the Townsend Press vocabulary series is *Advanced Word Power*. There are also short versions of the *Building, Improving,* and *Advancing* books, one of which is this book, *Building Vocabulary Skills, Short Version, Third Edition.* Suggested grade levels for the books are included in the *Instructor's Manual.* Together, the books can help create a vocabulary foundation that will make any student a better reader, writer, and thinker.

NOTES ON THE THIRD EDITION

A number of changes have been made in the third edition of *Building Vocabulary Skills, Short Version:*

- Material on how to solve word analogies has been added to the introduction, and a new unit test consisting of twenty word analogies has been prepared for each unit in the book. These tests provide practice in a format widely used in standardized tests.

- The remaining unit tests have been extensively revised, and a new multiple-choice section, using the words in realistic situations, has been added to Test 1 throughout.

- A new section, "Topics for Discussion and Writing," provides six high-interest items for each of the vocabulary chapters. Each item uses one or more of the vocabulary words in the chapter in a brief scenario suitable for class or small-group discussion, writing, or both.

- Finally, a number of practice items throughout the book have been revised or updated to ensure that each item works as clearly and effectively with students as possible.

ACKNOWLEDGMENTS

We are grateful for the enthusiastic comments provided by users of the Townsend Press vocabulary books over the life of the first and second editions. We appreciate as well the additional material provided by Beth Johnson and Susan Gamer; the editing work of Eliza Comodromos; the proofreading work of Barbara Solot; and, especially, the organizational, design, and editing skills of the indefatigable Janet M. Goldstein.

Sherrie L. Nist   *Carole Mohr*

Introduction

WHY VOCABULARY DEVELOPMENT COUNTS

You have probably often heard it said, "Building vocabulary is important." Maybe you've politely nodded in agreement and then forgotten the matter. But it would be fair for you to ask, "*Why* is vocabulary development important? Provide some evidence." Here are four compelling kinds of evidence.

1   Common sense tells you what many research studies have shown as well: vocabulary is a basic part of reading comprehension. Simply put, if you don't know enough words, you are going to have trouble understanding what you read. An occasional word may not stop you, but if there are too many words you don't know, comprehension will suffer. The content of textbooks is often challenge enough; you don't want to work as well on understanding the words that express that content.

2   Vocabulary is a major part of almost every standardized test, including reading achievement tests, college entrance exams, and armed forces and vocational placement tests. Test developers know that vocabulary is a key measure of both one's learning and one's ability to learn. It is for this reason that they include a separate vocabulary section as well as a reading comprehension section. The more words you know, then, the better you are likely to do on such important tests.

3   Studies have indicated that students with strong vocabularies are more successful in school. And one widely known study found that a good vocabulary, more than any other factor, was common to people enjoying successful careers in life. Words are in fact the tools not just of better reading, but of better writing, speaking, listening, and thinking as well. The more words you have at your command, the more effective your communication can be, and the more influence you can have on the people around you.

4   In today's world, a good vocabulary counts more than ever. Far fewer people work on farms or in factories. Far more are in jobs that provide services or process information. More than ever, words are the tools of our trade: words we use in reading, writing, listening, and speaking. Furthermore, experts say that workers of tomorrow will be called on to change jobs and learn new skills at an ever-increasing pace. The keys to survival and success will be the abilities to communicate skillfully and learn quickly. A solid vocabulary is essential for both of these skills.

Clearly, the evidence is overwhelming that building vocabulary is crucial. The question then becomes, "What is the best way of going about it?"

WORDS IN CONTEXT: THE KEY TO VOCABULARY DEVELOPMENT

Memorizing lists of words is a traditional method of vocabulary development. However, a person is likely to forget such memorized lists quickly. Studies show that to master a word, you must see and use it in various contexts. By working actively and repeatedly with a word, you greatly increase the chance of really learning it.

The following activity will make clear how this book is organized and how it uses a words-in-context approach. Answer the questions or fill in the missing words in the spaces provided.

Inside Front Cover and Contents

Turn to the inside front cover.

- The inside front cover provides a _____ that will help you pronounce all the vocabulary words in the book.

Now turn to the table of contents on pages v–vi.

- How many chapters are in the book? _____

- Four sections follow the last chapter. The first of these sections provides a limited answer key, the second gives helpful information on using _____, the third contains _____ _____, and the fourth is an index of the 200 words in the book.

Vocabulary Chapters

Turn to Chapter 1 on pages 8–11. This chapter, like all the others, consists of five parts:

- The *first part* of the chapter, on pages 8–9, is titled _____.

    The left-hand column lists the ten words. Under each **boldfaced** word is its _____ (in parentheses). For example, the pronunciation of *acknowledge* is _____. For a guide to pronunciation, see the inside front cover as well as "Dictionary Use" on page 131.

    Below the pronunciation guide for each word is its part of speech. The part of speech shown for *acknowledge* is _____. The vocabulary words in this book are mostly nouns, adjectives, and verbs. **Nouns** are words used to name something—a person, place, thing, or idea. Familiar nouns include *boyfriend, city, hat,* and *truth.* **Adjectives** are words that describe nouns, as in the following word pairs: *former* boyfriend, *large* city, *red* hat, *whole* truth. All of the **verbs** in this book express an action of some sort. They tell what someone or something is doing. Common verbs include *sing, separate, support,* and *imagine.*

    To the right of each word are two sentences that will help you understand its meaning. In each sentence, the **context**—the words surrounding the boldfaced word—provides clues you can use to figure out the definition. There are four common types of context clues—examples, synonyms, antonyms, and the general sense of the sentence. Each is briefly described below.

    1 Examples

    A sentence may include examples that reveal what an unfamiliar word means. For instance, take a look at the following sentence from Chapter 1 for the word *drastic*:

    The company's new president took **drastic** steps, closing two factories and laying off three hundred employees.

    The sentence provides two examples of steps that are drastic—the closing of two factories and the laying off of three hundred employees. To figure out what *drastic* means in that sentence, think about those examples. What kind of steps are being described? Look at the answer choices below, and in the answer space provided, write the letter of the one you feel is correct.

___ *Drastic* means   a. unimportant.   b. extreme.   c. easy.

Since the steps being described in the sentence are rather severe, or *extreme*, you probably guessed —correctly—that answer *b* is the right choice.

2 Synonyms

Synonyms are words that mean the same or almost the same as another word. For example, the words *joyful, happy*, and *delighted* are synonyms—they all mean about the same thing. Synonyms serve as context clues by providing the meaning of an unknown word that is nearby. The sentence below from Chapter 1 provides a synonym clue for *appropriate.*

Although it is **appropriate** for a man to take his hat off in a church, in a synagogue it is proper for a man to cover his head.

Rather than repeat *appropriate* in the second part of the sentence, the author used a synonym. Find that synonym, and then choose the letter of the correct answer from the choices below.

___ *Appropriate* means   a. illegal.   b. fun.   c. proper.

In the sentence from Chapter 1, *proper* is used as a synonym for *appropriate*. Both words refer to what is considered correct.

3 Antonyms

Antonyms are words with opposite meanings. For example, *help* and *harm* are antonyms, as are *work* and *rest*. Antonyms serve as context clues by providing the opposite meaning of an unknown word. The sentence below from Chapter 1 for the word *comply* provides an antonym clue.

If someone with an iron pipe demands your wallet, it is safer to **comply** than to resist.

To make a point, the author used an antonym of *comply*. Find the antonym, and then choose the letter below of the meaning of *comply*.

___ *Comply* means   a. to argue.   b. to do as asked.   c. to hear.

The sentence includes two reactions to being asked for your wallet: *to comply* and *to resist*. Since we can guess that *to comply* is probably the opposite of *to resist*, we can conclude that *comply* means "to do as asked."

4 General Sense of the Sentence

Even when there is no example, synonym, or antonym clue in a sentence, you can still figure out the meaning of an unfamiliar word. For example, look at the sentence from Chapter 1 for the word *acknowledge.*

Even after most of the votes had been counted, Senator Rice refused to **acknowledge** that he had lost.

After studying the context carefully, you should be able to choose the meaning of *acknowledge* from the three options presented. Write the letter of your choice.

___ *Acknowledge* means   a. to deny.   b. to admit.   c. to remember.

From the general sense of the sentence above, we can guess that the senator refused "to admit" that he had lost.

By looking closely at the pair of sentences provided for each word, as well as the answer choices, you should be able to decide on the meaning of a word. As you figure out each meaning, you are working actively with the word. You are creating the groundwork you need to understand and to remember the word. *Getting involved with the word and developing a feel for it, based upon its use in context, is the key to word mastery.*

It is with good reason, then, that the directions at the top of page 8 tell you to use the context to figure out each word's _____. Doing so deepens your sense of the word and prepares you for the next activity.

• The *second part* of the chapter, on page 9, is titled _____.

According to research, it is not enough to see a word in context. At a certain point, it is helpful as well to see the meaning of a word. The matching test provides that meaning, but it also makes you look for and think about that meaning. In other words, it continues the active learning that is your surest route to learning and remembering a word.

Note the caution that follows the test. Do not proceed any further until you are sure that you know the correct meaning of each word as used in context.

Keep in mind that a word may have more than one meaning. In fact, some words have quite a few meanings. (If you doubt it, try looking up in a dictionary, for example, the word *make* or *draw*.) In this book, you will focus on one common meaning for each vocabulary word. However, many of the words have additional meanings. For example, in Chapter 1, you will learn that *avert* means "to prevent," as in the sentence "Stop signs avert accidents." If you then look up *avert* in the dictionary, you will discover that it has another meaning—"to turn away," as in "The suspect averted her head to avoid being recognized." After you learn one common meaning of a word, you will find yourself gradually learning its other meanings in the course of your school and personal reading.

• The *third part* of the chapter, on page 10, is titled _____.

Here are ten sentences that give you an opportunity to apply your understanding of the ten words. After inserting the words, check your answers in the limited key at the back of the book. Be sure to use the answer key as a learning tool only. Doing so will help you to master the words and to prepare for the last two activities and the unit tests, for which answers are not provided.

• The *fourth and fifth parts* of the chapter, on pages 10–11, are titled _____ and _____.

Each practice tests you on all ten words, giving you two more chances to deepen your mastery. In the fifth part, you have the context of an entire passage in which you can practice applying the words.

At the bottom of the last page of this chapter is a box where you can enter your score for the final two checks. These scores should also be entered into the vocabulary performance chart located on the inside back page of the book. To get your score, take 10% off for each item wrong. For example, 0 wrong = 100%. 1 wrong = 90%, 2 wrong = 80%, 3 wrong = 70%, 4 wrong = 60%, and so on.

You now know, in a nutshell, how to proceed with the words in each chapter. Make sure that you do each page very carefully. *Remember that as you work through the activities, you are learning the words.*

How many times in all will you use each word? If you look, you'll see that each chapter gives you the opportunity to work with each word six times. Each "impression" adds to the likelihood that the word will become part of your active vocabulary. You will have further opportunities to use the word in the crossword puzzle and unit tests that end each unit and on the computer disks that are available with the book.

In addition, many of the words are repeated in context in later chapters of the book. Such repeated words are marked with small circles. For example, which words from Chapter 1 are repeated in the Final Check on page 15 of Chapter 2?

_____   _____

Analogies

This book also offers practice in word analogies, yet another way to deepen your understanding of words. An **analogy** is a similarity between two things that are otherwise different. Doing an analogy question is a two-step process. First you have to figure out the relationship in a pair of words. Those words are written like this:

LEAF : TREE

What is the relationship between the two words above? The answer can be stated like this: A leaf is a part of a tree.

Next, you must look for a similar relationship in a second pair of words. Here is how a complete analogy question looks:

LEAF : TREE ::

a. pond : river
c. page : book

b. foot : shoe
d. beach : sky

And here is how the question can be read:

___ LEAF is to TREE as

a. *pond* is to *river.*
c. *page* is to *book.*

b. *foot* is to *shoe.*
d. *beach* is to *sky.*

To answer the question, you have to decide which of the four choices has a relationship similar to the first one. Check your answer by seeing if it fits in the same wording as you used to show the relationship between *leaf* and *tree:* A ___ is part of a ___. Which answer do you choose?

The correct answer is *c.* Just as a *leaf* is part of a *tree,* a *page* is part of a *book.* On the other hand, a *pond* is not part of a *river,* nor is a *foot* part of a *shoe,* nor is a *beach* part of the *sky.*

We can state the complete analogy this way: *Leaf* is to *tree* as *page* is to *book.*

Here's another analogy question to try. Begin by figuring out the relationship between the first two words.

___ COWARD : HERO ::

a. soldier : military
c. actor : famous

b. infant : baby
d. boss : worker

Coward and *hero* are opposite types of people. So you need to look at the other four pairs to see which has a similar relationship. When you think you have found the answer, check to see that the two words you chose can be compared in the same way as *coward* and *hero:* ___ and ___ are opposite types of people.

In this case, the correct answer is *d; boss* and *worker* are opposite kinds of people. (In other words, *coward* is to *hero* as *boss* is to *worker.*)

By now you can see that there are basically two steps to doing analogy items:

1) Find out the relationship of the first two words.
2) Find the answer that expresses the same type of relationship as the first two words have.

Now try one more analogy question on your own. Write the letter of the answer you choose in the space provided.

___ SWING : BAT ::

a. drive : car
c. catch : bat

b. run : broom
d. fly : butterfly

If you chose answer *a,* you were right. *Swing* is what we do with a *bat,* and *drive* is what we do with a *car.*

A FINAL THOUGHT

The facts are in. A strong vocabulary is a source of power. Words can make you a better reader, writer, speaker, thinker, and learner. They can dramatically increase your chances of success in school and in your job.

But words will not come automatically. They must be learned in a program of regular study. If you commit yourself to learning words, and you work actively and honestly with the chapters in this book, you will not only enrich your vocabulary—you will enrich your life as well.

Unit One

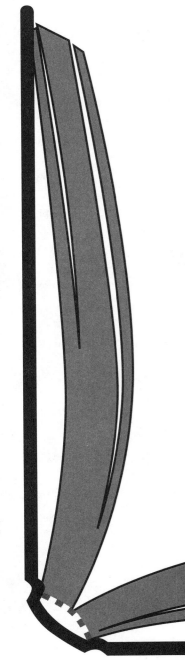

Chapter 1

acknowledge
alternative
anecdote
appropriate
avert

candid
compel
comply
concise
drastic

Chapter 2

dialog
erratic
extensive
forfeit
fortify

illuminate
isolate
refuge
reminisce
urban

Chapter 3

delete
impartial
integrity
legitimate
lenient

menace
morale
naive
overt
undermine

Chapter 4

endorse
erode
gruesome
hypocrite
idealistic

illusion
impact
imply
novice
obstacle

Chapter 5

concede
conservative
contrary
denounce
deter

disclose
scapegoat
superficial
sustain
transition

CHAPTER

1

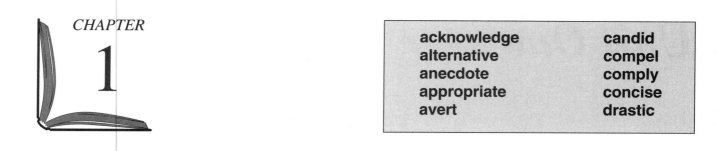

acknowledge	candid
alternative	compel
anecdote	comply
appropriate	concise
avert	drastic

Ten Words in Context

In the space provided, write the letter of the meaning closest to that of each **boldfaced** word. Use the context of the sentences to help you figure out each word's meaning.

1 acknowledge
(ăk-nŏl′ij)
-*verb*

- Stubborn people often find it difficult to **acknowledge** their errors. They hate to admit they were wrong.
- Even after most of the votes had been counted, Senator Rice refused to **acknowledge** that he had lost.

__ *Acknowledge* means   a. to deny.   b. to admit.   c. to remember.

2 alternative
(ôl-tûr′nə-tĭv)
-*noun*

- The teacher stated the **alternatives** to Tim—retake the test or get a D for the course.
- When her dog began to suffer from cancer, Wanda felt she had no **alternative**. He would have to be put to sleep.

__ *Alternative* means   a. a choice.   b. a command.   c. an assignment.

3 anecdote
(ăn′ĭk-dōt′)
-*noun*

- Dad told the children an **anecdote** about getting his tie caught in a file cabinet at work just as the boss walked in.
- I once heard an **anecdote** about a stagehand's revenge on a bossy actor. The stagehand put wheels on a table used in the play, so when the actor leaped onto the table during the most dramatic scene, he rolled straight off into the wings.

__ *Anecdote* means   a. an error.   b. a short, interesting story.   c. an article.

4 appropriate
(ə-prō′prē-ĭt)
-*adjective*

- Chuck has little sense of what is socially **appropriate**. For example, he went to his sister's wedding in running shoes.
- Although it is **appropriate** for a man to take his hat off in church, in a synagogue it is proper for a man to cover his head.

__ *Appropriate* means   a. illegal.   b. fun.   c. proper.

5 avert
(ə-vûrt′)
-*verb*

- Renata **averted** an unpleasant meeting with her ex-boyfriend by leaving the store before he saw her.
- To **avert** an accident, Larry turned his car sharply to the right and ran into a stop sign.

__ *Avert* means   a. to begin.   b. to prevent.   c. to report.

6 candid
(kăn′dĭd)
-*adjective*

- I'll give you my **candid** opinion, but you may not like what you hear.
- My heart always sinks when Robbie invites me to his house for dinner. He's a wonderful person, but to be **candid**, he's a terrible cook.

__ *Candid* means   a. honest.   b. friendly.   c. careful.

7 compel
(kəm-pĕl′)
-verb

- My history teacher would often **compel** us to do useless work, such as memorizing the date each state entered the union.
- If the law did not **compel** people to pay taxes, no one would pay them.

___ *Compel* means   a. to help.   b. to forbid.   c. to force.

8 comply
(kəm-plī′)
-verb

- If someone with an iron pipe demands your wallet, it is safer to **comply** than to resist.
- "My wife is so used to being the boss at work," Martin said, "that she is annoyed when I don't **comply** with her every request at home."

___ *Comply* means   a. to argue.   b. to do as asked.   c. to hear.

9 concise
(kŏn-sīs′)
-adjective

- Because of limited space, most newspaper articles must be **concise**.
- Unlike many politicians, our mayor is **concise**—his speeches are short but say much.

___ *Concise* means   a. wordy.   b. correct.   c. clear and brief.

10 drastic
(drăs′tĭk)
-adjective

- The company's new president took **drastic** steps, closing two factories and laying off three hundred employees.
- "This time I will let you off with just an hour of staying after school," the principal said. "But if it happens again, the punishment will be more **drastic**."

___ *Drastic* means   a. unimportant.   b. extreme.   c. easy.

Matching Words with Definitions

Following are definitions of the ten words. Clearly write or print each word next to its definition. The sentences above and on the previous page will help you decide on the meaning of each word.

1. _____   To do as commanded or asked

2. _____   Proper; suitable to the situation

3. _____   A choice

4. _____   Extreme; harsh or intense

5. _____   To admit or confess

6. _____   To force

7. _____   Very honest

8. _____   An entertaining short story about an event

9. _____   Saying much in a few clear words

10. _____   To prevent; to avoid

CAUTION: Do not go any further until you are sure the above answers are correct. Then you can use the definitions to help you in the following practices. Your goal is eventually to know the words well enough so that you don't need to check the definitions at all.

➤ Sentence Check 1

Using the answer line provided, complete each item below with the correct word from the box. Use each word once.

a. acknowledge	b. alternative	c. anecdote	d. appropriate	e. avert
f. candid	g. compel	h. comply	i. concise	j. drastic

_____ 1. Because Frank seems so ___, everyone believes him even when he tells a lie.

_____ 2. The drummer told interesting ___s about famous rock singers he had played for.

_____ 3. People often take ___ steps in anger, and they later regret their extreme actions.

_____ 4. When he saw no way to ___ the plane crash, the pilot parachuted to safety.

_____ 5. In a traditional wedding, the clergyman or clergywoman is often wordy, while the bride and groom are very ___, saying just "I do."

_____ 6. Any player who does not ___ with the rules will be dropped from the team.

_____ 7. A couple of older boys tried to ___ some first-graders to hand over their lunch money.

_____ 8. To earn money for college, Theo felt he had to either join the army or get a job. He didn't like either ___.

_____ 9. When the real ax-murderer confessed, the police had to ___ that the wrong man had been jailed.

_____ 10. In most American schools, it is not ___ for students to call their teachers by their first names.

NOTE: Now check your answers to these questions by turning to page 129. Going over the answers carefully will help you prepare for the next two practices, for which answers are not given.

➤ Sentence Check 2

Using the answer lines provided, complete each item below with **two** words from the box. Use each word once.

_____
_____ 1–2. "I ___ that you have a perfect right to do whatever you like with your hair," said the teenage girl's mother. "But, to be ___, I don't find green curls attractive."

_____
_____ 3–4. In colonial America, it was thought ___ for a wife to ___ with all her husband's commands.

_____
_____ 5–6. "The poor economic situation leaves me no ___," said the company president. "It ___s me to lay off some of our workers."

_____ 7–8. Our business instructor told an ___ about a company that ___(e)d failure by sharing ownership with all its workers.

_____

_____ 9–10. The sale sign was huge but ___. It said only, "___ price cuts."

_____

➤ _Final Check:_ Taking Exams

Here is a final opportunity for you to strengthen your knowledge of the ten words. First read the following selection carefully. Then fill in each blank with a word from the box at the top of the previous page. (Context clues will help you figure out which word goes in which blank.) Use each word once.

There are four test-taking methods to consider when faced with exams. The first is to impress your teachers with very clever answers. For example, you might respond to any question beginning with the word "Why" with a simple, (1)_____ reply: "Why not?" This is not recommended, however, unless you know that your instructor has a remarkable sense of humor. A second method is to try to reason your way out of taking the exam at all. You might try writing something like, "Should teachers (2)_____ students to take tests? Doesn't this go against our great American tradition of freedom? Besides, anyone who wants answers to these questions can find the information on the Internet." This method should not be used unless you are in (3)_____ need, as it involves a great deal of risk. It is (4)_____ only if you have shown yourself to be very brilliant throughout the course and you are the teacher's pet. Otherwise, you can expect your teacher to fail you. A third way of dealing with a test is to be (5)_____ and admit helplessness. According to one (6)_____, a student openly (7)_____(e)d ignorance by writing, "Only God knows the answer to this question." Unfortunately, the instructor's response was, "God gets an A. You get an F." The fact is, none of these three methods works very well. If you truly want to (8)_____ failure, you have no (9)_____ — you must (10)_____ with school rules. The fourth method is the only sure-fire one for dealing with exams: _study hard and learn the material._

Scores	Sentence Check 2 _____%	Final Check _____%

Enter your scores above and in the vocabulary performance chart on the inside back cover of the book.

CHAPTER

2

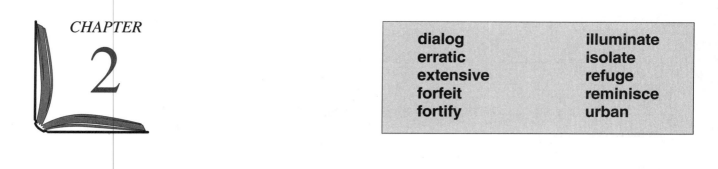

dialog	illuminate
erratic	isolate
extensive	refuge
forfeit	reminisce
fortify	urban

Ten Words in Context

In the space provided, write the letter of the meaning closest to that of each **boldfaced** word. Use the context of the sentences to help you figure out each word's meaning.

1 dialog
(dī′ə-lŏg′)
-noun

- The movie was shown with English subtitles because all its **dialog** was in French.
- At the PTA meeting last night, a **dialog** between parents and the faculty helped to clear up some differences between them.

__ *Dialog* means   a. a title.   b. a conversation.   c. an action.

2 erratic
(ĭ-răt′ĭk)
-adjective

- Children's eating habits are **erratic**. One day they'll barely eat, and the next day they'll eat enough for three.
- The driver ahead of me was **erratic**—he kept changing his speed and his lane.

__ *Erratic* means   a. noisy.   b. healthy.   c. irregular.

3 extensive
(ĕk-stĕn′sĭv)
-adjective

- Selina did **extensive** research for her paper—it took her several weeks.
- To save the wounded police officer, doctors performed **extensive** surgery that lasted for hours.

__ *Extensive* means   a. done quickly.   b. risky.   c. large in amount.

4 forfeit
(fôr′fĭt)
-verb

- The basketball players were upset when the team bus broke down and they had to **forfeit** an important game.
- If Phil damages his parents' car again, he will **forfeit** the right to drive it any more.

__ *Forfeit* means   a. to give up.   b. to win.   c. to ignore.

5 fortify
(fôr′tə-fī′)
-verb

- The night before running a marathon, Elsa **fortifies** herself by eating a large plate of pasta.
- The builders plan to **fortify** the old tower with steel beams.

__ *Fortify* means   a. to relax.   b. to strengthen.   c. to prove.

6 illuminate
(ĭ-lōō′mə-nāt′)
-verb

- Before electricity, streets were **illuminated** by gaslight.
- On Halloween, we made our trick-or-treat rounds with a flashlight to **illuminate** the way.

__ *Illuminate* means   a. to lose.   b. to clean.   c. to light up.

7 isolate
(ī′sə-lāt′)
-verb

- I thought I would enjoy **isolating** myself at the vacation cabin, but I soon felt lonely.
- Freddy was such a troublemaker that the teacher put his desk in a far corner to **isolate** him from the other students.

__ *Isolate* means   a. to protect.   b. to separate.   c. to recognize.

8 refuge
(rĕf′yōoj)
-noun

- A motorcycle offers no **refuge** in bad weather.
- My boyfriend and I first met when we took **refuge** in the same doorway during a sudden rain.

__ *Refuge* means   a. a shelter.   b. transportation.   c. a reason.

9 reminisce
(rĕm′ə-nĭs′)
-verb

- On their wedding anniversary, Lenny and Jean **reminisced** about their first date.
- My father showed me his trophy and **reminisced** about his years as a star basketball player.

__ *Reminisce* means   a. to remember.   b. to forget.   c. to ask.

10 urban
(ûr′bən)
-adjective

- Skyscrapers make for tightly packed **urban** populations. For example, some 16,000 people work in the Sears Tower in Chicago.
- Gladys likes **urban** living because she grew up in the city, but Emilio, who grew up on a farm, prefers country life.

__ *Urban* means   a. country.   b. city.   c. national.

Matching Words with Definitions

Following are definitions of the ten words. Clearly write or print each word next to its definition. The sentences above and on the previous page will help you decide on the meaning of each word.

1. _____   To light up

2. _____   To lose through some fault; to be forced to give up by way of penalty

3. _____   Shelter; protection

4. _____   Of or in a city

5. _____   A conversation; the conversation between characters in a story, novel, or play

6. _____   To separate from others

7. _____   Large in space or amount

8. _____   To strengthen

9. _____   To remember and talk about the past

10. _____   Not consistent

CAUTION: Do not go any further until you are sure the above answers are correct. Then you can use the definitions to help you in the following practices. Your goal is eventually to know the words well enough so that you don't need to check the definitions at all.

➤ *Sentence Check 1*

Using the answer line provided, complete each item below with the correct word from the box. Use each word once.

a. **dialog**	b. **erratic**	c. **extensive**	d. **forfeit**	e. **fortify**
f. **illuminate**	g. **isolate**	h. **refuge**	i. **reminisce**	j. **urban**

_____ 1. The skater's ___ performances showed that she was too inconsistent to hire for the ice show.

_____ 2. In London during World War II, bomb shelters provided ___ from air attacks.

_____ 3. Vitamins and minerals ___ the body against disease.

_____ 4. Politicians who are caught taking bribes ___ their good names.

_____ 5. Criminals are put in prison to ___ them from the rest of society.

_____ 6. The night before graduation, my roommate Gary and I ___(e)d about our four years together.

_____ 7. The pioneers used candles to ___ book pages at night.

_____ 8. The author's ___ was always sharp and bare: "You love me?" "Uh-huh." "Good."

_____ 9. Before his parents visit him, Don gives his apartment a(n) ___ cleaning; he dusts or scrubs every surface.

_____ 10. There's a big difference between a(n) ___ sky and a country sky. In the country, there are no bright lights to block the starlight.

NOTE: Now check your answers to these questions by turning to page 129. Going over the answers carefully will help you prepare for the next two practices, for which answers are not given.

➤ *Sentence Check 2*

Using the answer lines provided, complete each item below with **two** words from the box. Use each word once.

_____
_____ 1–2. The loud celebrating on the Fourth of July is so ___ in my neighborhood that the only place I find ___ from the noise is my basement.

_____
_____ 3–4. Curt ___(e)d for hours, revealing that his life had been very ___. At some points in his life, he was very busy, married, and well off. At other times, he lived alone and was out of work.

_____
_____ 5–6. Because criminals work in darkness, one way to reduce ___ crime would be to ___ streets and playgrounds with brighter lights.

_____ 7–8. To keep the opposing army from trying to ___ his weaker force
_____ the rest of the unit, the general decided to ___ his defenses.

_____ 9–10. In a ___ with the boss, several employees learned that they would ___
_____ their bonuses if they kept coming to work late.

➤ *Final Check:* Nate the Woodsman

Here is a final opportunity for you to strengthen your knowledge of the ten words. First read the following selection carefully. Then fill in each blank with a word from the box at the top of the previous page. (Context clues will help you figure out which word goes in which blank.) Use each word once.

Nate had spent most of his seventy years in the woods. As a young man, he had the alternative° of working in the city with his brother. But he decided that (1)_____ life was not for him. He preferred to (2)_____ himself from others and find (3)_____ in nature from the crowds and noise of the city. He was more than willing to (4)_____ such advantages as flush toilets and electric blankets for the joy of watching a sunrise (5)_____ the frozen pines.

Because Nate had lived alone for so long, his behavior was (6)_____. For example, one minute he'd be very quiet, and the next he'd (7)_____ at length about his youth. His knowledge of nature was (8)_____, and so I learned much from him through the years.

I will tell you an anecdote° that shows how wise he was about the woods and how miserly he could be with words. One evening Nate, my cousin Arthur, and I were crossing a meadow. Arthur's interest in some little white mushrooms that were growing there led to this (9)_____:

"These mushrooms look so good," said Arthur. "Did you ever use them, Nate?"

"Yep," said Nate. "My ma used to cook 'em up."

"Great!" said Arthur. Nate's words seemed to (10)_____ Arthur's desire for those mushrooms. He gathered about a hundred of them. "How'd she fix them?" he asked Nate.

"Cooked 'em up in sugar water."

"Really? And then you ate them that way?"

"Ate 'em?" Nate was horrified. "You crazy? We used to put 'em in a bowl on the table to kill flies!"

Scores	Sentence Check 2 _____%	Final Check _____%	

Enter your scores above and in the vocabulary performance chart on the inside back cover of the book.

delete	menace
impartial	morale
integrity	naive
legitimate	overt
lenient	undermine

Ten Words in Context

In the space provided, write the letter of the meaning closest to that of each **boldfaced** word. Use the context of the sentences to help you figure out each word's meaning.

1 delete
(dĭ-lēt′)
-*verb*

- When I accidentally **deleted** several paragraphs of my research paper from the computer, it took ten minutes to retype them.
- The invitation list is too long. Unless we **delete** a few names, the party will be too crowded.

__ *Delete* means   a. to type.   b. to add.   c. to erase.

2 impartial
(ĭm-pär′shəl)
-*adjective*

- Too much publicity before a trial makes it difficult for lawyers to find **impartial** jurors, people with no opinion about the case.
- "I'm an **impartial** judge of character," Dolores joked. "I distrust all people equally, without prejudice."

__ *Impartial* means   a. not whole.   b. fair.   c. friendly.

3 integrity
(ĭn-tĕg′rə-tē)
-*noun*

- Our boss trusts Ramon with the key to the cash register because she knows that he has **integrity**.
- I thought our senator had **integrity**, so I was shocked to hear that she had taken a bribe.

__ *Integrity* means   a. honesty.   b. talent.   c. a good memory.

4 legitimate
(lĕ-jĭt′ə-mĭt)
-*adjective*

- "A need to see the final episode in your favorite soap opera," said the teacher, "is not a **legitimate** excuse for missing class."
- Any company that guarantees to make all investors millionaires can't possibly be **legitimate**.

__ *Legitimate* means   a. safe.   b. considered proper.   c. healthy.

5 lenient
(lē′nē-ənt)
-*adjective*

- Ms. Hall is very **lenient** about late papers. If you hand one in even a week late, she doesn't lower your grade.
- Mom wouldn't let us feed our poodle during dinner. But Dad, who was more **lenient**, would look the other way when we slipped the dog something under the table.

__ *Lenient* means   a. heartless.   b. easygoing.   c. honest.

6 menace
(mĕn′ĭs)
-*noun*

- Acid rain is the biggest **menace** to the survival of freshwater fish.
- Ron's impatient attitude and his fast, zigzag driving make him a **menace** on the road.

__ *Menace* means   a. a puzzle.   b. something noticeable.   c. a danger.

7 morale
(mə-răl′)
-*noun*

- Art class was good for Tyrone's **morale**. Each time the teacher praised his drawings, his confidence and enthusiasm increased.
- The workers' **morale** was so low that they constantly complained about the job. Only going home could cheer them up.

__ *Morale* means   a. spirit.   b. pay.   c. sense of right.

8 naive
(nä-ēv′)
-*adjective*

- Though young, Rhoda is not **naive**. Being on her own for so long has made her streetwise.
- Having had little experience with salespeople, my younger sister is so **naive** that she believes everything they tell her.

__ *Naive* means   a. lacking experience.   b. generous.   c. questioning.

9 overt
(ō-vûrt′)
-*adjective*

- Sometimes **overt** racism is easier to deal with than the hidden kind. You can better fight what is out in the open.
- Martha's love of reading was **overt**—books spilled over the shelves in every room of her apartment.

__ *Overt* means   a. obvious.   b. fair.   c. harmful.

10 undermine
(ŭn′dər-mīn′)
-*verb*

- Leroy tried to **undermine** the coach's authority by making jokes about him behind his back.
- Numerous floods had **undermined** the foundation so greatly that the house was no longer safe.

__ *Undermine* means   a. to reach.   b. to explore.   c. to weaken.

Matching Words with Definitions

Following are definitions of the ten words. Clearly write or print each word next to its definition. The sentences above and on the previous page will help you decide on the meaning of each word.

1. _____   Fair; not biased; without prejudice

2. _____   A threat

3. _____   In accordance with accepted laws, rules, and standards

4. _____   State of mind with respect to confidence and enthusiasm; spirit

5. _____   To cross out or erase

6. _____   To gradually weaken or damage

7. _____   Obvious; not hidden

8. _____   Not strict or harsh in disciplining or punishing; merciful

9. _____   Lacking worldly experience; unsuspecting; unsophisticated

10. _____   Honesty; strong moral sense

CAUTION: Do not go any further until you are sure the above answers are correct. Then you can use the definitions to help you in the following practices. Your goal is eventually to know the words well enough so that you don't need to check the definitions at all.

➤ *Sentence Check 1*

Using the answer line provided, complete each item below with the correct word from the box. Use each word once.

a. **delete**	b. **impartial**	c. **integrity**	d. **legitimate**	e. **lenient**
f. **menace**	g. **morale**	h. **naive**	i. **overt**	j. **undermine**

_____ 1. When my brother and I argued, my mother remained ___. She didn't want to favor either of us.

_____ 2. Alison's repeated criticisms ___ her sister's self-confidence.

_____ 3. Drugs have become a terrible ___ to the well-being of America's children.

_____ 4. The team's ___ was high—the players were in good spirits and thought they would win the game.

_____ 5. Although advertising by doctors and lawyers was once considered improper, it is now ___.

_____ 6. My father is so ___ about business deals that he has been tricked by cheaters more than once.

_____ 7. Computers make it easy to ___ unwanted information from a report without having to type the report all over again.

_____ 8. Mrs. Dean's dislike for the mayor was ___. She stood right up in front of the crowd and called him a two-faced liar.

_____ 9. "The boss is ___ the first time an employee makes a mistake," Sherry's coworker warned, "but he's very strict the second time."

_____ 10. Mark Twain once joked that he had even more ___ than George Washington. "Washington could not lie," he said. "I can, but I won't."

NOTE: Now check your answers to these questions by turning to page 129. Going over the answers carefully will help you prepare for the next two practices, for which answers are not given.

➤ *Sentence Check 2*

Using the answer lines provided, complete each item below with **two** words from the box. Use each word once.

_____
_____ 1–2. Nick's interest in Janice's money is ___ enough for all her friends to notice. But Janice is so ___ that she has no idea about the real reason for Nick's attention.

_____
_____ 3–4. The employees' ___ quickly fell when they learned that some of the company's earnings were put into a business that was not ___ and that was being investigated by the police.

_____
_____ 5–6. To give her essay ___, Isabel ___d some statements that were not entirely true.

_____   7–8. Donald is a real ___ in the classroom. It's not uncommon for him to
_____   ___ classroom order by shooting little spitballs at other students.

_____   9–10. My parents should be ___, but they're much more ___ with my sisters
_____   than with me. My sisters often get off with a scolding. In contrast, I'm
                                    often compelled° to stay home for a night.

➤ *Final Check:* **Who's on Trial?**

Here is a final opportunity for you to strengthen your knowledge of the ten words. First read the following
selection carefully. Then fill in each blank with a word from the box at the top of the previous page.
(Context clues will help you figure out which word goes in which blank.) Use each word once.

It would be nice to think every trial involved a(n) (1)_____ judge and
jury who wanted only to decide a case fairly. However, we would be (2)_____
to believe the world is always fair and just. Two famous trials in history show us that when
accusers have no (3)_____ charges, they sometimes invent some.

The first trial is that of Socrates, a teacher in ancient Greece. Socrates did not give lectures or
write books. Instead, he wandered around the marketplace in Athens, starting a discussion with
anyone he met. Socrates was a man of great (4)_____: he lived an honest life in
search of truth. But by pointing out the faults of some upper-class Athenians, he made enemies.
The Greek authorities feared he would (5)_____ their ability to rule. Eventually
Socrates was arrested and tried for being a(n) (6)_____ to the youth of Athens.
He was found guilty and sentenced to death. His friends urged him to escape, but Socrates said he
had to comply° with the court's decree. He carried out the sentence by drinking a cup of poison.

Jesus of Nazareth was another teacher who lived a life of great honesty. He, too, frightened the
authorities of his time. More and more people flocked to hear the words of this carpenter who
spoke of God as a loving father. Afraid he might encourage people to turn against them, the
authorities invented charges against him. They said he hurt the (7)_____ of the
country, making people unhappy and restless. The authorities' illegal treatment of Jesus was
(8)_____: they allowed no lawyer or advisers to help him; they took him from
his friends late at night, beat him, and dragged him into court the next morning. He was brought
before the Roman governor Pontius Pilate. Pilate made some attempt to be (9)_____
with Jesus, at one point telling the crowd, "I find no guilt in this man." However, Pilate lacked the
courage to act on his belief. He had Jesus beaten yet again and sent him to be executed.

The evidence is clear and should not be (10)_____(e)d from the history
books: In some trials, society itself is the guilty party.

| *Scores* | Sentence Check 2 _____% | Final Check _____% |

Enter your scores above and in the vocabulary performance chart on the inside back cover of the book.

endorse	illusion
erode	impact
gruesome	imply
hypocrite	novice
idealistic	obstacle

Ten Words in Context

In the space provided, write the letter of the meaning closest to that of each **boldfaced** word. Use the context of the sentences to help you figure out each word's meaning.

1 **endorse**
(ĕn-dôrs′)
-*verb*

- "If you **endorse** the new shopping mall," said the speaker, "you're supporting a large increase in neighborhood traffic."
- Some athletes earn more money **endorsing** such products as cereal and sneakers than they do playing their sport.

__ *Endorse* means   a. to buy.   b. to support.   c. to see.

2 **erode**
(ĭ-rōd′)
-*verb*

- As water **eroded** the topsoil, the tree roots beneath it became more and more visible.
- The team's confidence in its coach was **eroded** by his increasingly wild accusations against its opponents.

__ *Erode* means   a. to wear away.   b. to build up.   c. to escape.

3 **gruesome**
(grōō′səm)
-*adjective*

- The automobile accident was so **gruesome** that I had to look away from the horrible sight.
- The young campers sat around the fire and scared each other with **gruesome** horror stories.

__ *Gruesome* means   a. unfair.   b. boring.   c. frightening.

4 **hypocrite**
(hĭp′ə-krĭt′)
-*noun*

- Dominic is such a **hypocrite**. He cheats his customers yet complains about how hard it is to be an honest, struggling salesman.
- I feel that the worst **hypocrites** are those who preach love and then attack anyone of a different culture or faith.

__ *Hypocrite* means   a. an insincere person.   b. a religious person.   c. a loud person.

5 **idealistic**
(ī-dē′ə-lĭs′tĭk)
-*adjective*

- Very **idealistic** people are drawn to professions like teaching or the ministry, in which they feel they can help make the world a better place.
- My sister is too **idealistic** ever to marry for wealth or fame—she would marry only for love.

__ *Idealistic* means   a. full of ideas.   b. emphasizing ideals.   c. young.

6 **illusion**
(ĭ-lōō′zhən)
-*noun*

- People lost in the desert sometimes experience the **illusion** that there is a lake right in front of them.
- The idea that the sun sets and rises is an **illusion**. It is really the earth that is turning away from and then toward the sun.

__ *Illusion* means   a. a fact.   b. a new idea.   c. a false impression.

7 impact
(ĭm′păkt)
-*noun*

- When birds accidentally fly into windows, the **impact** of hitting the glass often kills them.
- That boxer punches with such power that the **impact** of his uppercut can knock out most opponents.

___ *Impact* means   a. a force.   b. a possibility.   c. a sight.

8 imply
(ĭm-plī′)
-*verb*

- To Sherlock Holmes, the clues **implied** that the murderer was an elderly man who carried a cane.
- When my friend asked me, "Do you feel all right?" she **implied** that I did not look well.

___ *Imply* means   a. to hide.   b. to overlook.   c. to suggest.

9 novice
(nŏv′ĭs)
-*noun*

- Because my father has never played tennis, he will join the class for **novices**.
- "Don't buy an expensive camera for a **novice**," said the saleswoman. "Let your son first get some experience with a cheap camera."

___ *Novice* means   a. a child.   b. a beginner.   c. a friend.

10 obstacle
(ŏb′stə-kəl)
-*noun*

- I'd better clean my apartment soon. There are too many **obstacles** on the floor between my bed and the refrigerator.
- The major **obstacle** to Hal's getting a promotion is his laziness.

___ *Obstacle* means   a. something hidden.   b. something helpful.   c. something that gets in the way.

Matching Words with Definitions

Following are definitions of the ten words. Clearly write or print each word next to its definition. The sentences above and on the previous page will help you decide on the meaning of each word.

1. _____   To express indirectly; suggest

2. _____   Something that gets in the way; a barrier

3. _____   One who claims to be something he or she is not; an insincere person

4. _____   A false impression; a mistaken view of reality

5. _____   To support; express approval of; to state in an ad that one supports a product or service, usually for a fee

6. _____   Horrible; shocking; frightful

7. _____   A beginner; someone new to a field or activity

8. _____   The force of one thing striking another

9. _____   To gradually wear (something) away

10. _____   Tending to emphasize ideals and principles over practical concerns

CAUTION: Do not go any further until you are sure the above answers are correct. Then you can use the definitions to help you in the following practices. Your goal is eventually to know the words well enough so that you don't need to check the definitions at all.

➤ *Sentence Check 1*

Using the answer line provided, complete each item below with the correct word from the box. Use each word once.

a. **endorse**	b. **erode**	c. **gruesome**	d. **hypocrite**	e. **idealistic**
f. **illusion**	g. **impact**	h. **imply**	i. **novice**	j. **obstacle**

_____ 1. The horror movie became too ___ when the monster started eating people.

_____ 2. Year after year, the waves continue to ___ the beach, wearing it away by constantly beating against it.

_____ 3. Poems often ___ an idea. That is, they hint at the idea rather than state it directly.

_____ 4. I was such a(n) ___ at computers that I didn't even know how to insert a disk.

_____ 5. Karen is the least ___ person I know. She is guided only by a desire to get ahead.

_____ 6. Don't be such a(n) ___! If you don't like Arlene, then you shouldn't pretend that you do.

_____ 7. An actress hired to ___ meat products on TV was fired when it was learned she was a vegetarian.

_____ 8. Ballet dancers sometimes break their toes when they land with too great a(n) ___ after a leap.

_____ 9. We can never drive straight into our driveway because there are always ___s there—tricycles, garbage cans, or toys.

_____ 10. When the moon is low in the sky, it looks much larger than when it is overhead. This difference in size, however, is only a(n) ___.

NOTE: Now check your answers to these questions by turning to page 129. Going over the answers carefully will help you prepare for the next two practices, for which answers are not given.

➤ *Sentence Check 2*

Using the answer lines provided, complete each item below with **two** words from the box. Use each word once.

_____
_____ 1–2. "Just because I let them meet in the church basement," said Reverend Lucas, "does not ___ that I ___ everything the group stands for."

_____
_____ 3–4. When the first soldier to fly in an airplane took off in 1908, he had no ___ about the danger, but he never expected to die from the ___ of crashing into a cemetery wall.

_____   5–6. The first Peace Corps volunteers may have been ___, but they were
_____   tough about their dreams. No ___ would keep them from working for a
                                          better world.

_____   7–8. Because she was just out of college, Faye was a(n) ___ at interviewing
_____   job applicants. Nevertheless, she could see that Perry was a(n) ___ who
                                          boasted about job skills he didn't have.

_____   9–10. Ten years in the soil had ___(e)d the body down to a mere skeleton.
_____   But when a gardener's shovel uncovered the ___ remains of the murder
                                          victim, she could still be identified by a gold locket around her neck.

➤ _Final Check:_ Night Nurse

Here is a final opportunity for you to strengthen your knowledge of the ten words. First read the following
selection carefully. Then fill in each blank with a word from the box at the top of the previous page.
(Context clues will help you figure out which word goes in which blank.) Use each word once.

    I'm no (1)_____, so I'll admit I wish I'd never taken the job of nurse on the

midnight shift in a hospital emergency room. Not a single person in my family would

(2)_____ my career decision, and maybe my family was right. I had no

(3)_____s about the difficulty of the work. I knew the emergency room

would be tough, but I wasn't going to let that be a(n) (4)_____. Still, I did

start out more (5)_____ about helping the world than I am now, ten

months later. I don't mean to (6)_____ that I've given up on nursing, because I

haven't. But when I first rushed a stretcher off an ambulance—as a(n) (7)_____

at the job—disappointment and regret had not yet started to (8)_____ my hopeful

outlook.

    I work at one of the biggest urban° hospitals in the state. More often than not, each shift brings

a series of (9)_____ injuries, caused by everything from shootings to

household accidents, but mostly by car crashes. One effect of my job has been to make me always

wear a seat belt—I've seen first-hand the damage caused by the (10)_____ of a

human head thrown against a windshield.

    Emergency-room workers seem to follow one of two routes. Either they become accustomed

to the difficult sights and stay in the field for years, or they quickly burn out and move into another

line of work. I'm in the second category. Next week, I'm applying for a job in a doctor's office.

Scores	Sentence Check 2 _____%	Final Check _____%

Enter your scores above and in the vocabulary performance chart on the inside back cover of the book.

concede	disclose
conservative	scapegoat
contrary	superficial
denounce	sustain
deter	transition

Ten Words in Context

In the space provided, write the letter of the meaning closest to that of each **boldfaced** word. Use the context of the sentences to help you figure out each word's meaning.

1 **concede**
(kən-sēd′)
-*verb*

- Our aunt hates to admit an error. She will never **concede** that she might be wrong.
- After pretending it was easy learning to use the new computer, Ross had to **concede** that he was struggling and ask for help.

__ *Concede* means   a. to forget.   b. to admit.   c. to prove.

2 **conservative**
(kən-sûr′və-tĭv)
-*adjective*

- Lauren's **conservative** relatives were shocked when she broke with tradition and wore a rose-colored wedding gown.
- When the mayor suggested a new method of recycling garbage, a **conservative** member of the audience called out, "What we've done in the past is good enough. Why change things?"

__ *Conservative* means   a. playful.   b. amused.   c. traditional.

3 **contrary**
(kŏn′trĕr-ē)
-*adjective*

- Claire's father insists that she share his views. He doesn't allow her to express an opinion **contrary** to his.
- Dale and her husband have **contrary** ideas on how to spend a vacation. He wants to sleep on the beach for a week, but she prefers visiting museums.

__ *Contrary* means   a. different.   b. favorable.   c. similar.

4 **denounce**
(dĭ-nouns′)
-*verb*

- In Nazi Germany, anyone who publicly **denounced** Hitler as cruel or mad risked imprisonment, torture, and death.
- When Eugene said he saw me steal from another student's locker, I **denounced** him as a liar.

__ *Denounce* means   a. to imitate.   b. to defend.   c. to condemn.

5 **deter**
(dĭ-tûr′)
-*verb*

- No one is sure how much the threat of capital punishment **deters** murder.
- Beth's parents disapproved of her dating someone from a different culture, but their prejudice didn't **deter** her—she still dated Po-Yen.

__ *Deter* means   a. to discourage.   b. to encourage.   c. to change.

6 **disclose**
(dĭs-klōz′)
-*verb*

- When I applied for financial aid, I had to **disclose** my family's annual income. But it embarrassed me to reveal this information.
- The police don't **disclose** all the facts of a murder to the newspapers. That way, there will be some information which only the murderer would know.

__ *Disclose* means   a. to reveal.   b. to deny.   c. to replace.

7 scapegoat
(skāp′gōt′)
-noun

- Several girls put dye into their high school swimming pool. In need of a **scapegoat**, they blamed another student who knew nothing about the prank.
- Because the manager wanted a **scapegoat** for his own mistake, he fired an innocent employee.

___ *Scapegoat* means   a. a correction.   b. a punishment.   c. someone to blame.

8 superficial
(soo′pər-físh′əl)
-adjective

- Sal and Anita are interested only in appearances. They are so **superficial** that it's impossible to have a deep friendship with them.
- My teacher said my essay on divorce was too **superficial** because I didn't go into the subject in detail.

___ *Superficial* means   a. lacking depth.   b. complicated.   c. satisfactory.

9 sustain
(sə-stān′)
-verb

- My diets usually last three days at the most. I can't **sustain** my willpower any longer than that.
- An opera singer can **sustain** a high note for a long period of time.

___ *Sustain* means   a. to remember.   b. to delay.   c. to continue.

10 transition
(trăn-zĭsh′ən)
-noun

- Mark's parents were amazed at how easily he made the **transition** from full-time student to full-time employee.
- "The **transition** from being childless to being a parent is extreme," said the new father. "Last week, only two quiet people lived at home. Suddenly, we have a third, noisy resident."

___ *Transition* means   a. an explanation.   b. a trip.   c. a change.

Matching Words with Definitions

Following are definitions of the ten words. Clearly write or print each word next to its definition. The sentences above and on the previous page will help you decide on the meaning of each word.

1. _____   Lacking depth or meaning; shallow

2. _____   Totally different; opposite; conflicting

3. _____   A change from one activity, condition, or location to another

4. _____   Someone blamed for the mistakes of others

5. _____   To admit to something

6. _____   To prevent or discourage

7. _____   To reveal; make known

8. _____   To openly condemn; express disapproval of

9. _____   To keep something going; continue

10. _____   Tending to resist change; favoring traditional values and views

CAUTION: Do not go any further until you are sure the above answers are correct. Then you can use the definitions to help you in the following practices. Your goal is eventually to know the words well enough so that you don't need to check the definitions at all.

➤ *Sentence Check 1*

Using the answer line provided, complete each item below with the correct word from the box. Use each word once.

a. **concede**	b. **conservative**	c. **contrary**	d. **denounce**	e. **deter**
f. **disclose**	g. **scapegoat**	h. **superficial**	i. **sustain**	j. **transition**

_____ 1. The teenagers who smashed the window made an innocent bystander a ___, claiming he had thrown the rock.

_____ 2. To ___ a high grade point average throughout college requires much studying.

_____ 3. The environmental group ___ (e)d a local chemical company for polluting the river.

_____ 4. Even after Stuart listed scientific facts that support his theory, the teacher refused to ___ that Stuart might be right.

_____ 5. A childhood stutter didn't ___ Leon. He overcame his speech handicap and reached his goal of being a radio announcer.

_____ 6. I try to judge people by their character, not by something as ___ as physical appearance.

_____ 7. Knowing my passion for chocolate, my mother refused to ___ the location of the bite-size Hershey bars, which she was saving for company.

_____ 8. Making the ___ from her own apartment to a nursing home has been difficult for my grandmother.

_____ 9. Though Geena and Tom are happily married, they cast ___ votes in almost every election—she's a Republican and he's a Democrat.

_____ 10. When Dawn brought home a boyfriend with purple hair and an earring, her ___ parents, who prefer everything old-fashioned and traditional, nearly fainted.

NOTE: Now check your answers to these questions by turning to page 129. Going over the answers carefully will help you prepare for the next two practices, for which answers are not given.

➤ *Sentence Check 2*

Using the answer lines provided, complete each item below with **two** words from the box. Use each word once.

_____
_____ 1–2. Starting with the ___ from home to college, some students neglect high school friendships which they had vowed always to ___.

_____
_____ 3–4. Stan is more interested in how much money people have than in who they are. He is a ___ person, and that quality ___s people from becoming his friends.

_____   5–6. The owners of the unsafe factory used their employees as ___s. They ___(e)d the workers, claiming that the explosion at the factory was entirely their fault.
_____

_____   7–8. Mayor Jones was ___, preferring traditional solutions. So it was hard for him to ___ that some of the extreme ideas of his opponent might work.
_____

_____   9–10. Once Sandy ___(e)d her true values in the course of our conversation, I realized they were quite ___ to what I had supposed. She was not the type of person that I had believed her to be.
_____

➤ *Final Check:* **Relating to Parents**

Here is a final opportunity for you to strengthen your knowledge of the ten words. First read the following selection carefully. Then fill in each blank with a word from the box at the top of the previous page. (Context clues will help you figure out which word goes in which blank.) Use each word once.

As I look back at my relationship with my parents, I realize that we have gone through an interesting cycle together. When I was a kid, my parents were everything to me—the smartest, most interesting, most loving people in the world. But when I turned 13, there was a drastic° change—I suddenly developed a very (1)_____ view of them. I thought they were unreasonably strict. While I loved everything new in music, hairstyles, and clothes, they seemed boringly (2)_____, wanting everything to remain the same. Our conversations, which used to be so deep and satisfying, became (3)_____ chats. I felt as if I had nothing to say to them anymore. If we (4)_____(e)d a conversation for any length of time, I quickly lost patience with what I considered their silly, old-fashioned ideas. To my friends, I often (5)_____(e)d them as hopelessly out of touch with the modern world.

But now, as I'm making the (6)_____ from my teen years to adulthood, I've had to (7)_____ that I was wrong. My parents are the same patient, loving, wise people they always were. I see that I used them as (8)_____s for my own uncertainties and for problems I had caused myself. I assumed they would not listen to opinions different from their own. Now I know that I can (9)_____ my plans and dreams to them, and they will listen with respect. I hope I will never again let my own interests (10)_____ me from recognizing my parents' genuine love and concern for me.

Scores   Sentence Check 2 _____%   Final Check _____%

Enter your scores above and in the vocabulary performance chart on the inside back cover of the book.

UNIT ONE: Review

The box at the right lists twenty-five words from Unit One. Using the clues at the bottom of the page, fill in these words to complete the puzzle that follows.

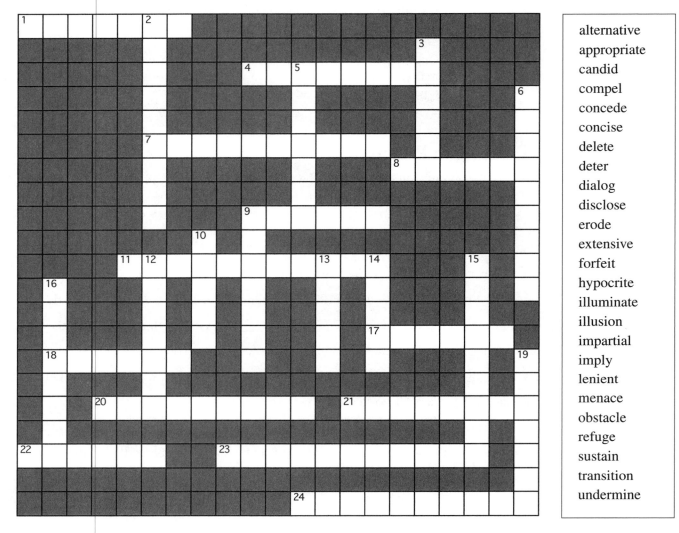

alternative
appropriate
candid
compel
concede
concise
delete
deter
dialog
disclose
erode
extensive
forfeit
hypocrite
illuminate
illusion
impartial
imply
lenient
menace
obstacle
refuge
sustain
transition
undermine

ACROSS

1. To lose through some fault; to be forced to give up by way of a penalty
4. Something that gets in the way; a barrier
7. A change from one activity, condition, or location to another
8. To cross out or erase
9. Very honest
11. A choice
17. A conversation; the conversation between characters in a story, novel or play
18. To force
20. Large in space or amount
21. A false impression; a mistaken view of reality
22. A threat
23. Proper; suitable to the situation
24. To light up

DOWN

2. Fair; not biased; without prejudice
3. Shelter; protection
5. To keep something going; continue
6. To gradually weaken or damage
9. To admit to something
10. To prevent or discourage
12. Not strict or harsh in disciplining or punishing
13. To express indirectly; suggest
14. To gradually wear (something) away
15. One who claims to be something he or she is not; an insincere person
16. To reveal; make known
19. Saying much in a few clear words

UNIT ONE: Test 1

PART A
Choose the word that best completes each item and write it in the space provided.

_____ 1. Smoking and drinking ___ your health.

    a. fortify   b. undermine   c. compel   d. isolate

_____ 2. To ___ disaster in river rafting, you must steer clear of rocks.

    a. avert   b. erode   c. compel   d. endorse

_____ 3. Damage to the old car was so ___ that repairs would have cost more than the car did.

    a. conservative   b. extensive   c. impartial   d. concise

_____ 4. The nurses asked the local union to ___ their strike by signing a letter of support.

    a. comply   b. undermine   c. endorse   d. isolate

_____ 5. After I failed my first two algebra quizzes, I decided that the sensible ___ to flunking was to get some tutoring.

    a. alternative   b. scapegoat   c. impact   d. morale

_____ 6. Although the movie is titled _Tears of Blood_, it isn't ___; it contains no violence or blood.

    a. erratic   b. candid   c. gruesome   d. idealistic

_____ 7. On the first day of school, the kindergarten students met their new teacher, a 21-year-old ___ who was probably more nervous than they were.

    a. hypocrite   b. novice   c. menace   d. refuge

_____ 8. One advantage of ___ living is the city's wealth of live entertainment, including plays and concerts.

    a. erratic   b. idealistic   c. candid   d. urban

_____ 9. One speaker spoke for over an hour, but Greg was ___, taking only ten minutes to make his points.

    a. drastic   b. erratic   c. naive   d. concise

_____ 10. At Gene's ten-year high-school reunion, he was struck by how many of his classmates seemed to have already made the ___ from a youthful to a middle-aged lifestyle.

    a. obstacle   b. illusion   c. transition   d. morale

(Continues on next page)

PART B
On the answer line, write the letter of the choice that best completes each item.

_____ 11. Although the pizza shop appeared to be **legitimate**, it in fact
    a. ran an illegal gambling business.   b. was not well-known.
    c. was losing money.   d. was busy and popular.

_____ 12. The **appropriate** response when someone says, "How are you?" is to
    a. remain silent.   b. say, "How am I what?"
    c. say, "Fine, thank you. And you?"   d. say, "It's none of your business."

_____ 13. Ross **conceded** to his boss that he had made the error, saying,
    a. "Sorry. My error."   b. "Lee did it."
    c. "That's not an error."   d. "You told me to do it."

_____ 14. Katya **sustained** her no-smoking effort by
    a. sneaking a smoke now and then.   b. saying, "I just can't quit!"
    c. picturing herself healthier each day.   d. being with people who smoke.

_____ 15. My mother **implied** that she didn't like my new haircut when she said,
    a. "You look terrific!"   b. "I hate your new haircut."
    c. "Whoever cut your hair is talented."   d. "Hmm, that's an interesting haircut."

_____ 16. If my brother were really **idealistic**, he would
    a. give me cash for my birthday.   b. spend more time doing volunteer work.
    c. find out which careers paid the most money.   d. get married.

_____ 17. A **conservative** politician
    a. is dishonest and can't be trusted.   b. favors extreme change.
    c. looks for ways to raise our taxes.   d. likes to do things the old-fashioned way.

_____ 18. Jenna's dislike of Barry is **overt**; she
    a. insults him openly whenever she sees him.
    b. pretends to like him.
    c. likes most things about him, but a few things bother her.
    d. can't understand why she dislikes him.

_____ 19. We are **compelled** to
    a. relax at the end of a day.
    b. apologize whenever we hurt someone's feelings.
    c. volunteer to help the homeless.
    d. stop the car we're driving at red lights and stop signs.

_____ 20. When I came poorly prepared for my piano lesson, my teacher's **candid** comment was
    a. "You waste your money on lessons if you don't practice."
    b. "You're making excellent progress."
    c. "You're ready to go on to a new piece."
    d. "In music, practice is not important."

**Score**   (Number correct) _____ x 5 = _____ %

UNIT ONE: Test 2

PART A
Complete each item with a word from the box. Use each word once.

a. acknowledge	b. delete	c. denounce	d. dialog	e. disclose
f. drastic	g. fortify	h. hypocrite	i. integrity	j. isolate
k. morale	l. refuge	m. reminisce		

_____ 1. The old wooden beams in the barn were so weak that we had to ___ them with metal rods.

_____ 2. Prisoners of war may be tortured until they are willing to publicly ___ their own governments.

_____ 3. In the 1870s one man took ___ action when his wife refused to serve him breakfast: he divorced her.

_____ 4. Americans ___ that they have a great fear of cancer. When surveyed, most report that they fear this disease more than any other.

_____ 5. There is no hunting in the state park, which serves as a(n) ___ for wildlife.

_____ 6. In order to make viewers tune in the next day, soap opera episodes often end just before a character ___s some shocking secret.

_____ 7. ___ is so low in my father's office that he comes home depressed almost every night.

_____ 8. When a formerly top-secret document was shown on TV, all names and places were ___(e)d. As a result, nearly every sentence had gaps.

_____ 9. People who work alone in toll booths must often feel their job ___s them too much, especially late at night.

_____ 10. Westerns are shown throughout the world. Still, it's odd to think of cowboys speaking their ___ in German, French, or Japanese.

_____ 11. Dominic has ___. When he accidentally backed into a parked car and smashed one of its lights, he was honest enough to leave a note with his name and number.

_____ 12. That woman is a(n) ___. She gives speeches about the evils of cruelty to animals but eats meat and owns two fur coats.

_____ 13. I listened to my grandparents ___ about all the crazy fads they've seen come and go, including T-shirts that gave off a smell of chocolate, garlic, or fish when scratched.

(Continues on next page)

PART B

Write **C** if the italicized word is used **correctly**. Write **I** if the word is used **incorrectly**.

_____ 14. The *impact* of the baseball was so great that my hand stung even though I was wearing a mitt.

_____ 15. In seventeenth-century Massachusetts, one *lenient* jury hanged a dog accused of being a witch.

_____ 16. My little sister is *naive* about basketball. She knows the names and records of dozens of players.

_____ 17. Since he wanted to borrow the car that night, Harry decided to *comply* with his mother's request that he clean his room.

_____ 18. Whenever my brother makes a mistake, he blames someone else. He loves being the *scapegoat*.

_____ 19. *Impartial* employers often prejudge young job applicants as likely to be inexperienced.

_____ 20. Once he laid eyes on the mint-condition Corvette, nothing could *deter* Paolo from his goal of owning the car.

_____ 21. Alaskan wolves are not a *menace* to humans—they don't attack people.

_____ 22. The candidate was happy to see his support among factory workers start to *erode*.

_____ 23. Cesar's moodiness makes his work *erratic*. One week he's a top salesman, and the next week he can't seem to sell a thing.

_____ 24. Professor Wise gained his *superficial* knowledge of the mating and parenting habits of bedbugs through years of research.

_____ 25. In fifth-century France and Spain, a doctor was required to leave a cash deposit before caring for a patient. If the patient lived, the doctor got his money back. If the patient died, the doctor *forfeited* the deposit.

Score (Number correct) _____ x 4 = _____%

UNIT ONE: Test 3

PART A: Synonyms
In the space provided, write the letter of the choice that is most nearly the **same** in meaning as the **boldfaced** word.

_____ 1. **refuge**   a) argument   **b)** shelter   c) denial   **d)** schedule

_____ 2. **endorse**   a) support   **b)** build   c) reveal   **d)** think over

_____ 3. **urban**   a) mild   **b)** in a city   c) noisy   **d)** up-to-date

_____ 4. **alternative**   a) lack of interest   **b)** memory   c) choice   **d)** insides

_____ 5. **deter**   a) encourage   **b)** find   c) prevent   **d)** enter

_____ 6. **impact**   a) agreement   **b)** force   c) danger   **d)** chance

_____ 7. **obstacle**   a) vehicle   **b)** aid   c) decision   **d)** barrier

_____ 8. **imply**   a) obey   **b)** state clearly   c) attract   **d)** suggest

_____ 9. **conservative**   a) traditional   **b)** cruel   c) modern   **d)** to the point

_____ 10. **hypocrite**   a) one new to a field   **b)** supporter   c) opponent   **d)** insincere person

_____ 11. **reminisce**   a) remember   **b)** do again   c) look forward to   **d)** overlook

_____ 12. **compel**   a) register   **b)** require   c) comfort   **d)** allow

_____ 13. **concede**   a) admire   **b)** hide   c) admit   **d)** strengthen

_____ 14. **drastic**   a) extreme   **b)** usual   c) rare   **d)** strict

_____ 15. **idealistic**   a) young   **b)** seeing the worst   c) happy   **d)** emphasizing ideals

_____ 16. **novice**   a) fictional character   **b)** beginner   c) protector   **d)** one who takes

_____ 17. **scapegoat**   a) farmer   **b)** laborer   c) planner   **d)** one blamed for others' mistakes

_____ 18. **illusion**   a) reality   **b)** false view   c) fame   **d)** lighting

_____ 19. **transition**   a) change   **b)** hope   c) information   **d)** criticism

_____ 20. **morale**   a) design   **b)** accident   c) spirit   **d)** struggle

_____ 21. **anecdote**   a) story   **b)** falsehood   c) cure   **d)** argument

_____ 22. **avert**   a) insist   **b)** award   c) promote   **d)** avoid

_____ 23. **dialog**   a) argument   **b)** literary conversation   c) mistaken view   **d)** disguise

_____ 24. **integrity**   a) combination   **b)** wisdom   c) honesty   **d)** image

_____ 25. **forfeit**   a) prevent   **b)** do as asked   c) forget   **d)** lose

(Continues on next page)

PART B: Antonyms

In the space provided, write the letter of the choice that is most nearly the **opposite** in meaning to the **boldfaced** word.

_____ 26. **naive**   a) experienced   b) having ideals   c) hidden   d) insincere

_____ 27. **comply**   a) enter   b) disobey   c) agree   d) build up

_____ 28. **illuminate**   a) support   b) compete against   c) avoid   d) darken

_____ 29. **menace**   a) female   b) correct view   c) protection   d) harm

_____ 30. **acknowledge**   a) admit   b) convince   c) deny   d) forget

_____ 31. **legitimate**   a) illegal   b) experienced   c) united   d) not chosen

_____ 32. **extensive**   a) praised   b) small   c) improper   d) biased

_____ 33. **lenient**   a) well-known   b) educational   c) deep   d) strict

_____ 34. **candid**   a) dishonest   b) wordy   c) unusual   d) unfriendly

_____ 35. **overt**   a) beginning   b) extreme   c) mild   d) hidden

_____ 36. **denounce**   a) praise   b) weaken   c) compete   d) announce

_____ 37. **sustain**   a) recognize   b) assist   c) discontinue   d) decorate

_____ 38. **impartial**   a) welcome   b) biased   c) elderly   d) strange

_____ 39. **appropriate**   a) famous   b) inconvenient   c) forgotten   d) improper

_____ 40. **undermine**   a) strengthen   b) find   c) describe   d) criticize

_____ 41. **fortify**   a) eat   b) build   c) weaken   d) entertain

_____ 42. **superficial**   a) expensive   b) deep   c) capable   d) legal

_____ 43. **erratic**   a) experienced   b) not required   c) for sale   d) consistent

_____ 44. **concise**   a) short   b) young   c) wordy   d) honest

_____ 45. **isolate**   a) unite   b) state   c) allow   d) interrupt

_____ 46. **delete**   a) add   b) reject   c) fix   d) encourage

_____ 47. **erode**   a) define   b) allow   c) build up   d) empty

_____ 48. **gruesome**   a) obvious   b) reduced   c) necessary   d) pleasant

_____ 49. **contrary**   a) valuable   b) similar   c) consistent   d) surprised

_____ 50. **disclose**   a) forget   b) approve   c) prevent   d) hide

Score   (Number correct) _____ x 2 = _____ %

Enter your score above and in the vocabulary performance chart on the inside back cover of the book.

UNIT ONE: *Test 4*

Each item below starts with a pair of words in CAPITAL LETTERS. For each item, figure out the relationship between these two words. Then decide which of the choices (*a*, *b*, *c*, or *d*) expresses a similar relationship. Write the letter of your choice on the answer line.

_____ 1. ANECDOTE : TELL ::

    a. lecture : sing   b. television : delay
    c. letter : write   d. garden : read

_____ 2. CONCISE : WORDY ::

    a. apologize : explain   b. exist : live
    c. offer : suggest   d. arrive : leave

_____ 3. CANDID : HONESTY ::

    a. joyful : pain   b. powerful : strength
    c. doubtful : certainty   d. confused : smoke

_____ 4. DRASTIC : HARSH ::

    a. frightening : scary   b. late : later
    c. difficult : simple   d. different : interesting

_____ 5. DIALOG : CONVERSATION ::

    a. telephone : e-mail   b. radio : book
    c. letter : envelope   d. lecture : speech

_____ 6. ERRATIC : IRREGULAR ::

    a. unusual : often   b. odd : typical
    c. expected : event   d. unexpected : surprising

_____ 7. ILLUMINATE : LIGHTBULB ::

    a. water : oil   b. paint : picture
    c. heat : furnace   d. cool : mixer

_____ 8. REFUGE : BOMB SHELTER ::

    a. dwelling : apartment   b. airport : traveler
    c. train : station   d. mosque : religion

_____ 9. DELETE : INSERT ::

    a. erase : cross out   b. pronounce : word
    c. outline : write   d. subtract : add

_____ 10. MENACE : RECKLESS DRIVER ::

    a. danger : loaded gun   b. medicine : common cold
    c. food : plastic bag   d. rescue : shark attack

(Continues on next page)

_____ 11. MORALE : TEAM ::

    a. navy : army   b. group : family

    c. goodwill : business   d. arrow : goal

_____ 12. OVERT : HIDDEN ::

    a. valuable : worthless   b. over : above

    c. immediate : quick   d. educational : program

_____ 13. ERODE : WEAR AWAY ::

    a. create : imagine   b. push : pull

    c. assist : help   d. view : enjoy

_____ 14. GRUESOME : HORROR MOVIE ::

    a. colorful : garden   b. heavy : newspaper

    c. final : beginning   d. quiet : airport

_____ 15. ILLUSION : MAGICIAN ::

    a. textbook : student   b. dinner : chef

    c. election : candidate   d. movie : audience

_____ 16. OBSTACLE : OVERCOME ::

    a. detour : ignore   b. target : miss

    c. movie : delay   d. puzzle : solve

_____ 17. CONTRARY : SIMILAR ::

    a. confusing : clear   b. conflicting : clashing

    c. opposite : different   d. heated : argument

_____ 18. DISCLOSE : CONCEAL ::

    a. close : shut   b. know : remember

    c. continue : stop   d. discover : explore

_____ 19. SCAPEGOAT : BLAME ::

    a. movie star : fame   b. bird : robin

    c. aunt : cousin   d. soldier : sailor

_____ 20. SUPERFICIAL : MAKEUP::

    a. healthful : sugar   b. welcome : illness

    c. deep : ocean   d. fatal : twisted ankle

Score   (Number correct) _____ x 5 = _____%

Unit Two

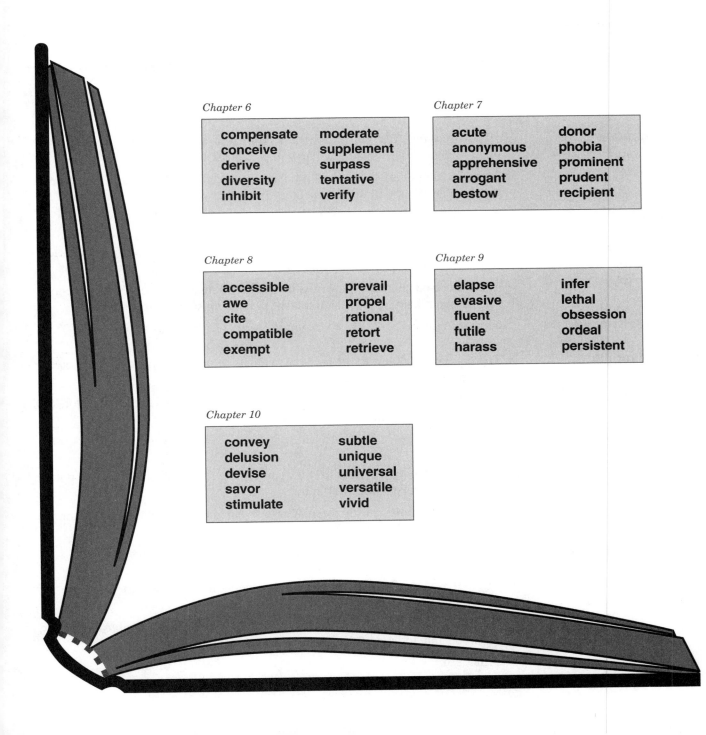

Chapter 6

compensate	moderate
conceive	supplement
derive	surpass
diversity	tentative
inhibit	verify

Chapter 7

acute	donor
anonymous	phobia
apprehensive	prominent
arrogant	prudent
bestow	recipient

Chapter 8

accessible	prevail
awe	propel
cite	rational
compatible	retort
exempt	retrieve

Chapter 9

elapse	infer
evasive	lethal
fluent	obsession
futile	ordeal
harass	persistent

Chapter 10

convey	subtle
delusion	unique
devise	universal
savor	versatile
stimulate	vivid

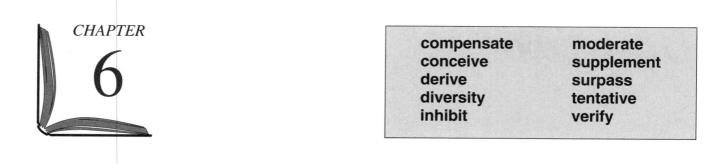

compensate	moderate
conceive	supplement
derive	surpass
diversity	tentative
inhibit	verify

Ten Words in Context

In the space provided, write the letter of the meaning closest to that of each **boldfaced** word. Use the context of the sentences to help you figure out each word's meaning.

1 **compensate**
(kŏm′pən-sāt′)
-verb

- Some companies still don't **compensate** women for their work as much as they pay men who do the same or similar work.
- When an oil rig explosion killed Sam, the company **compensated** his widow with $100,000. However, nothing could really repay her for his loss.

___ *Compensate* means   a. to notice.   b. to pay.   c. to hire.

2 **conceive**
(kən-sēv′)
-verb

- When studying Australia in school, I **conceived** an interesting class project—each student could write to an Australian pen pal.
- Most people in the 1800s could not have imagined such things as TV and heart transplants. What will the next century bring that we cannot yet **conceive** of?

___ *Conceive* means   a. to think of.   b. to expect.   c. to remember.

3 **derive**
(dĭ-rīv′)
-verb

- We **derive** plastics from oil. As a result, when oil prices go up, so do the prices of plastic products.
- Sarah **derived** pleasure from visiting and reading to old people after school. She enjoyed their company and felt she was doing something worthwhile.

___ *Derive* means   a. to recognize.   b. to get.   c. to want.

4 **diversity**
(dĭ-vûr′sĭ-tē)
-noun

- There's a great **diversity** of breakfast cereals at the supermarket. There are so many different kinds that they take up half an aisle.
- "One thing I'm looking for in a college," Sandra told her counselor, "is **diversity**. I want to meet many different kinds of people."

___ *Diversity* means   a. sameness.   b. need.   c. variety.

5 **inhibit**
(ĭn-hĭb′ĭt)
-verb

- Steve wanted to drive fast in his new car, but the fact that he had already gotten two speeding tickets **inhibited** him.
- Many people believe exercise makes one eat more, but I find that exercise **inhibits** my urge to snack.

___ *Inhibit* means   a. to hold back.   b. to get into the habit.   c. to satisfy.

6 **moderate**
(mŏd′ər-ĭt)
-adjective

- The trail was neither flat nor extremely steep—it was **moderate**, suitable for the average hiker.
- The prices at this restaurant aren't dirt cheap, but they are **moderate**. So we should be able to have a nice dinner without spending too much.

___ *Moderate* means   a. modern.   b. average.   c. difficult.

7 supplement
(sŭp′lə-mənt)
-verb

- Many people **supplement** their diet with vitamins.
- At busy times of the year, the department store **supplements** its sales staff with temporary workers.

___ *Supplement* means   a. to replace.   b. to add to.   c. to reduce.

8 surpass
(sər-păs′)
-verb

- You can reach and even **surpass** many of your highest goals.
- Denise was disappointed that she had only matched Rhonda's record leap in the high jump—she had hoped to **surpass** it.

___ *Surpass* means   a. to go beyond.   b. to avoid.   c. to equal.

9 tentative
(tĕn′tə-tĭv)
-adjective

- My parents' wedding anniversary party date is **tentative**. Before we finalize the date, we have to be sure that everyone can be with us that weekend.
- Class membership was **tentative** because many students were still dropping and adding courses.

___ *Tentative* means   a. clear.   b. not definite.   c. early.

10 verify
(vĕr′ə-fī′)
-verb

- Race officials **verified** who the winner was by checking a photo of the horses at the finish line.
- We'd love to come to the party, but I have to check my calendar to **verify** that we're free that evening.

___ *Verify* means   a. to predict.   b. to deny.   c. to check.

Matching Words with Definitions

Following are definitions of the ten words. Clearly write or print each word next to its definition. The sentences above and on the previous page will help you decide on the meaning of each word.

1. _____   Variety

2. _____   To make suitable payment to; pay; repay

3. _____   To do better than; go beyond in achievement or quality

4. _____   To test or check the truth or accuracy of something; prove

5. _____   To add to, especially to make up for a lack

6. _____   To receive from a source; get

7. _____   Not definite; not final

8. _____   Medium; average; not extreme in quality, degree, or amount

9. _____   To think of; imagine

10. _____   To hold back; prevent

CAUTION: Do not go any further until you are sure the above answers are correct. Then you can use the definitions to help you in the following practices. Your goal is eventually to know the words well enough so that you don't need to check the definitions at all.

➤ *Sentence Check 1*

Using the answer line provided, complete each item below with the correct word from the box. Use each word once.

a. **compensate**	b. **conceive**	c. **derive**	d. **diversity**	e. **inhibit**
f. **moderate**	g. **supplement**	h. **surpass**	i. **tentative**	j. **verify**

_____ 1. The Mississippi River ___s its name from Indian words meaning "big river."

_____ 2. To ___ that his checkbook balance was correct, Craig added the numbers again.

_____ 3. If you aren't very hungry, then take only a ___ helping of food.

_____ 4. The exact cast of the movie remains ___ until it is known whether or not Tom Cruise is available.

_____ 5. Babe Ruth's record number of home runs in a single baseball season was ___(e)d first by Roger Maris, then by Mark McGwire in 1998, and most recently by Barry Bonds in 2001.

_____ 6. The Motor Vehicle Bureau now ___s its driver's manual with an attached publication on the new driving laws.

_____ 7. Even with her relatives, shy Yoko didn't feel free to be herself. Their noisy talk ___(e)d her.

_____ 8. Artists feel frustrated when what they ___ of in their minds fails to appear on the painted canvas.

_____ 9. "Hearing a ___ of opinions is fine," said Lynn. "But it would be nice if everyone in this family could agree once in a while."

_____ 10. When my uncle helped me pay for college, he said I could ___ him by helping someone else pay for college when I can afford to.

NOTE: Now check your answers to these questions by turning to page 129. Going over the answers carefully will help you prepare for the next two practices, for which answers are not given.

➤ *Sentence Check 2*

Using the answer lines provided, complete each item below with **two** words from the box. Use each word once.

_____
_____ 1–2. My sister cannot ___ of being in a relationship with someone who would ___ her personal growth.

_____
_____ 3–4. I have ___ plans to meet Cesar at the Midtown Theatre at eight, but first I have to ___ the show time and call him back.

_____
_____ 5–6. When the company offered to ___ its employees well for working on Saturdays, the number of volunteers ___(e)d all expectations.

_____ 7–8. I ___ great pleasure from having my paintings in an art show, and I can
_____   ___ my income by selling some of them.

_____ 9–10. City College offers a ___ of courses and majors at a ___ price. Many
_____   students don't realize they have an unusually wide choice of courses at
                                  a lower cost than at many other colleges.

➤ *Final Check:* Job Choices

Here is a final opportunity for you to strengthen your knowledge of the ten words. First read the following
selection carefully. Then fill in each blank with a word from the box at the top of the previous page.
(Context clues will help you figure out which word goes in which blank.) Use each word once.

After job-hunting for two months, Jessica had to choose between two alternatives° for

employment—a fashion magazine and a clothing store. She already had (1)_____

job offers from both employers. They planned to make the offers definite after they were able to

(2)_____ the information on her job application.

In the meanwhile, Jessica thought about the good and bad points of the two jobs. Both offered

the (3)_____ that she liked; she hated doing the same thing every day.

Both had good benefits, such as sick leave and vacation time. However, the two companies would

not (4)_____ her equally. At the clothing store, Jessica would start out at

a (5)_____ salary. With her many expenses, she might even have to find a

part-time job in the evenings to (6)_____ this salary. But there were other,

better points. Working for the store, Jessica would be free to put her many ideas into practice right

away. Her manager said he would not (7)_____ any attempts she might

make to move up in the company. In fact, he promised her that if her work was good, he would

endorse° a promotion for her himself within a few months. At the fashion magazine, Jessica's

starting salary would far (8)_____ what she would get paid at the

clothing store—she wouldn't have to worry about money at all, but promotions and raises were

not so likely. Jessica could (9)_____ of both jobs as learning experiences

and also felt she could (10)_____ much satisfaction from either one.

This would not be an easy decision.

Scores Sentence Check 2 _____%	Final Check _____%

Enter your scores above and in the vocabulary performance chart on the inside back cover of the book.

acute	donor
anonymous	phobia
apprehensive	prominent
arrogant	prudent
bestow	recipient

Ten Words in Context

In the space provided, write the letter of the meaning closest to that of each **boldfaced** word. Use the context of the sentences to help you figure out each word's meaning.

1 acute
(ə-kyōot′)
-*adjective*

• Gil joked, "This painting looks like something my two-year-old son would do." Then he felt **acute** regret when he learned the artist was standing behind him.

• My headache pains were so **acute** that they felt like needles in my head.

___ *Acute* means   a. very great.   b. mild.   c. slow.

2 anonymous
(ə-nŏn′ə-məs)
-*adjective*

• Many **anonymous** works are very famous. For example, the author of the Christmas carol "God Rest Ye Merry, Gentlemen" is unknown.

• Laura tore up an **anonymous** note that said that her teenage daughter had cheated on a test. "If the writer was too ashamed to sign the note," said Laura, "why should I believe it?"

___ *Anonymous* means   a. short.   b. having an unknown author.   c. poorly written.

3 apprehensive
(ăp′rĭ-hĕn′sĭv)
-*adjective*

• Ginny was **apprehensive** as she approached the cow, not knowing if it would try to bite or kick her.

• It is natural to be **apprehensive** when making a major purchase, such as a computer or a car. Only the very wealthy can afford not to be at all nervous at such times.

___ *Apprehensive* means   a. fearful.   b. irritated.   c. confident.

4 arrogant
(ăr′ə-gənt)
-*adjective*

• Having been a very spoiled child, Becky turned out to be a very **arrogant** grownup.

• One of the most **arrogant** people I know paid the state extra money to get a custom license plate that reads "IMBEST."

___ *Arrogant* means   a. polite.   b. quiet.   c. showing too much self-importance.

5 bestow
(bĭ-stō′)
-*verb*

• The Manhattan School of Music **bestowed** an honorary degree on a famous musician who had never gone to college.

• At the science fair, the judges **bestowed** the first prize on Vincent, whose experiment showed that dogs are colorblind.

___ *Bestow* means   a. to take.   b. to prepare.   c. to award.

6 donor
(dō′nər)
-*noun*

• Our soccer team is seeking **donors** to contribute money for new uniforms.

• The man's twin sister was the **donor** of his new kidney.

___ *Donor* means   a. one who receives.   b. one who gives.   c. one who doubts.

7 phobia
(fō′bē-ə)
-*noun*

- My roommate has joined a group that helps people with **phobias** because she wants to overcome her extreme fear of even the smallest spiders.
- Ned's fear of flying is so severe that he won't even step onto an airplane. But he says he's in no rush to cure his **phobia**, since driving is cheaper anyway.

___ *Phobia* means   a. an illness.   b. an extreme fear.   c. a bad temper.

8 prominent
(prŏm′ə-nənt)
-*adjective*

- Crystal's long black hair is so **prominent** that it's the first thing you notice about her.
- The Big Bird balloon was the most **prominent** one in the parade because it was so large and such a bright yellow.

___ *Prominent* means   a. very colorful.   b. expensive.   c. obvious.

9 prudent
(prōōd′ənt)
-*adjective*

- Sidney has learned the hard way that it's not **prudent** to tease our ill-tempered dog.
- **Prudent** as always, Meg thought carefully before finally deciding which of the used cars would be the best buy.

___ *Prudent* means   a. relaxed.   b. courageous.   c. careful and wise.

10 recipient
(rĭ-sĭp′ē-ənt)
-*noun*

- Katherine Hepburn was the **recipient** of an Academy Award for her role in *On Golden Pond* in 1981, almost fifty years after her first Academy Award.
- Doug was the annoyed **recipient** of fourteen pieces of junk mail on the same day.

___ *Recipient* means   a. one who gives.   b. one who receives.   c. one with good luck.

Matching Words with Definitions

Following are definitions of the ten words. Clearly write or print each word next to its definition. The sentences above and on the previous page will help you decide on the meaning of each word.

1. _____   A person who gives or contributes

2. _____   Frightened; uneasy; anxious

3. _____   A continuing, abnormally extreme fear of a particular situation or thing

4. _____   Cautious; careful; wise

5. _____   Severe; sharp

6. _____   Filled with self-importance; overly proud and vain

7. _____   Very noticeable; obvious

8. _____   A person who receives

9. _____   Created or given by an unknown or unidentified person

10. _____   To give, as an honor or a gift; award

CAUTION: Do not go any further until you are sure the above answers are correct. Then you can use the definitions to help you in the following practices. Your goal is eventually to know the words well enough so that you don't need to check the definitions at all.

➤ *Sentence Check 1*

Using the answer line provided, complete each item below with the correct word from the box. Use each word once.

a. **acute**	b. **anonymous**	c. **apprehensive**	d. **arrogant**	e. **bestow**
f. **donor**	g. **phobia**	h. **prominent**	i. **prudent**	j. **recipient**

_____ 1. Because of her ___, Martha will walk up twenty floors to avoid taking an elevator.

_____ 2. The unsigned letter to the editor was not published because it was the newspaper's policy never to print ___ letters.

_____ 3. Since I didn't eat all day, I began to feel ___ hunger pains in my stomach by early evening.

_____ 4. The secretary to the president of the company acts very ___. She thinks she's more important than the other secretaries.

_____ 5. Carla was so popular that each year she was the ___ of dozens of Valentines.

_____ 6. When he retires, the biology professor will ___ on the school his collection of animal skeletons.

_____ 7. "Your decision to wait to marry until after graduation seems ___ to me," Larry's father said, pleased that his son was acting so wisely.

_____ 8. Cliff became more and more ___ about his driver's test. He was afraid he'd forget to signal, fail to park correctly, or even get into an accident.

_____ 9. Because the new tax laws limit certain deductions, art museums have fewer ___s.

_____ 10. The most ___ plants in Denzel's garden are giant lilies. Some of them are eight feet tall.

NOTE: Now check your answers to these questions by turning to page 129. Going over the answers carefully will help you prepare for the next two practices, for which answers are not given.

➤ *Sentence Check 2*

Using the answer lines provided, complete each item below with **two** words from the box. Use each word once.

_____
_____ 1–2. The millionaire was so ___ that he refused to be a major ___ to the new town library unless it was named for him.

_____
_____ 3–4. It's ___ to keep medication on hand if anyone in the family is subject to ___ asthma attacks.

_____
_____ 5–6. Joey is very ___ when he has to give a speech in class, and his stutter becomes especially ___. As a result, he never raises his hand in class.

_____   7–8. The famous actress was sometimes the ___ of ___ letters from fans too
_____   shy to sign their names.

_____   9–10. Carlotta felt her therapist had ___ed upon her the greatest of gifts:
_____   freedom from fear of open spaces. Before her treatment, Carlotta's ___
                                 had kept her a prisoner in her own home. It had inhibited° her from
                                 even walking into her own front yard.

➤ _Final Check:_ Museum Pet

Here is a final opportunity for you to strengthen your knowledge of the ten words. First read the following
selection carefully. Then fill in each blank with a word from the box at the top of the previous page.
(Context clues will help you figure out which word goes in which blank.) Use each word once.

"I've got great news!" the museum director shouted as he ran into the employees' lunchroom.

"Someone wants to (1)_____ five million dollars on the museum."

"Who?" one staff member asked excitedly.

"I don't know. He wishes his gift to remain (2)_____. There's just one

obstacle°," he added.

The employees' smiles faded, and they began to look (3)_____.

"It seems our mystery (4)_____ has a strange (5)_____:

he's terribly afraid of cats."

Everyone turned to look at Willard, who had been the museum pet since he'd wandered in as a

tiny kitten more than five years ago. As usual, the big orange cat was stretched out in a

(6)_____ spot near the lunchroom entrance. He continued licking himself,

not aware that he was the (7)_____ of everyone's attention.

"I'm afraid Willard will have to go," the director said sadly. "This contributor isn't just a little

afraid of cats; his fear is really (8)_____. Apparently, he panicked when he

saw Willard the last time he came. We can't risk frightening him again. It just wouldn't be

(9)_____. Remember, he might give us more money in the future."

"I think it's pretty (10)_____ of this contributor, whoever he is, to ask us

to give up poor old Willard for him, even if he does want to give us the money," one employee said

angrily.

"I know you'll miss Willard," the director said, "but it would be a shame to forfeit° the money.
And I'll be glad to have him come live at my house. You can all visit him whenever you like." And
so Willard found a new home, where he still lives happily. The museum used the five million
dollars to build a new addition, which was known as the Willard Wing.

Scores	Sentence Check 2 _____%	Final Check _____%

Enter your scores above and in the vocabulary performance chart on the inside back cover of the book.

CHAPTER

8

accessible	prevail
awe	propel
cite	rational
compatible	retort
exempt	retrieve

Ten Words in Context

In the space provided, write the letter of the meaning closest to that of each **boldfaced** word. Use the context of the sentences to help you figure out each word's meaning.

1 accessible
(ăk-sĕs′ə-bəl)
-adjective

- The department store was not **accessible** from her side of the road, so Kristin looked ahead for a U-turn.
- We always hung the candy canes on the Christmas tree's highest branches, where they weren't **accessible** to the younger children.

___ *Accessible* means   a. good to look at.   b. within reach.   c. desirable.

2 awe
(ô)
-noun

- Frank and Donna have different types of idols. Although Frank greatly admires Michael Jordan, Donna is filled with **awe** for Mother Teresa.
- Sid is in **awe** of his gymnastics coach, whom he considers the greatest man he knows.

___ *Awe* means   a. anger.   b. respect.   c. hope.

3 cite
(sīt)
-verb

- Jeff was embarrassed but pleased when the teacher **cited** his essay as an example of good writing.
- Tired of picking up after her sister, Janet **cited** examples of her sloppiness: "stacks of papers, piles of dirty clothes, and unwashed dishes."

___ *Cite* means   a. to forget.   b. to mention.   c. to ignore.

4 compatible
(kəm-păt′ə-bəl)
-adjective

- My girlfriend and I weren't very **compatible**; whenever she wasn't angry with me, I was angry with her.
- Some sweet and salty foods are **compatible**: for example, chocolate-covered pretzels are yummy.

___ *Compatible* means   a. well-known.   b. healthy.   c. in agreement.

5 exempt
(ĭg-zĕmpt′)
-adjective

- Since he had never been spanked, my little brother thought he was **exempt** from punishment—until he wrote on the walls in ink.
- Students with A averages were **exempt** from final exams, so the top three students went to the shore while the rest of us sweated it out on exam day.

___ *Exempt* means   a. excused.   b. in fear.   c. hiding.

6 prevail
(prĭ-vāl′)
-verb

- Most Hollywood movies have a happy ending: good **prevails** over evil.
- Although Kennedy **prevailed** over Nixon in 1960, eight years later Nixon won the presidency.

___ *Prevail* means   a. to win.   b. to watch.   c. to lose.

7 propel
(prə-pĕl′)
-verb

- My brother gave me a shove, which **propelled** me into the lake fully clothed.
- When the wind failed to **propel** the boat, we lowered the sails and turned on the motor.

___ *Propel* means   a. to support.   b. to move forward.   c. to raise.

8 rational
(răsh′ə-nəl)
-adjective

- Mr. Tibbs isn't **rational**; in addition to believing he came from another planet, he does crazy things like shoveling snow in his pajamas.
- The belief that breaking a mirror brings seven years of bad luck isn't **rational**. The only bad luck it could really bring is stepping on a sharp piece of broken glass.

___ *Rational* means   a. helpful.   b. kind.   c. reasonable.

9 retort
(rĭ-tôrt′)
-noun

- Sue, who is slender, boasted, "Thin is in." So Pat, who is heavy, gave this **retort**: "Well, fat is where it's at."
- When Shelley's balding boyfriend made fun of her new perm, her **retort** was, "Jealous?"

___ *Retort* means   a. a wish.   b. an answer.   c. a fact.

10 retrieve
(rĭ-trēv′)
-verb

- My dog Floyd refuses to **retrieve** a thrown Frisbee. Instead of running to bring it back, he only tilts his head and gives me a questioning look.
- I can't **retrieve** my sweater from the library until tomorrow, since the library had closed by the time I realized the sweater was missing.

___ *Retrieve* means   a. to remember.   b. to touch.   c. to get back.

Matching Words with Definitions

Following are definitions of the ten words. Clearly write or print each word next to its definition. The sentences above and on the previous page will help you decide on the meaning of each word.

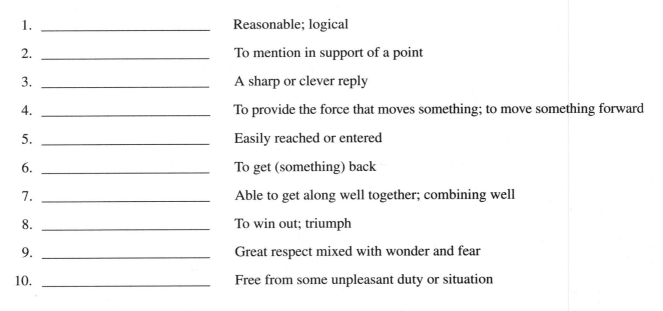

1. _____   Reasonable; logical

2. _____   To mention in support of a point

3. _____   A sharp or clever reply

4. _____   To provide the force that moves something; to move something forward

5. _____   Easily reached or entered

6. _____   To get (something) back

7. _____   Able to get along well together; combining well

8. _____   To win out; triumph

9. _____   Great respect mixed with wonder and fear

10. _____   Free from some unpleasant duty or situation

CAUTION: Do not go any further until you are sure the above answers are correct. Then you can use the definitions to help you in the following practices. Your goal is eventually to know the words well enough so that you don't need to check the definitions at all.

➢ *Sentence Check 1*

Using the answer line provided, complete each item below with the correct word from the box. Use each word once.

a. **accessible**	b. **awe**	c. **cite**	d. **compatible**	e. **exempt**
f. **prevail**	g. **propel**	h. **rational**	i. **retort**	j. **retrieve**

_____ 1. When I go bowling with Joan, she usually wins, but I always ___ in Scrabble.

_____ 2. Jet engines ___ a plane forward.

_____ 3. I ran back to the ladies' room to ___ my purse, but someone had already taken it.

_____ 4. In my family, a person is ___ from household chores on his or her birthday.

_____ 5. The cabinet above the refrigerator was ___ to Janet but not to her roommate Mieko, who was much shorter.

_____ 6. The general's uniform and medals filled Scott with ___. However, Marla, who knew the general personally, felt only disrespect for him.

_____ 7. My father thinks everything combines well with peanut butter. He even thinks peanut butter and onions are ___ in a sandwich.

_____ 8. When Bridget writes up her experiment, she will ___ similar studies by other researchers, to show that her results match theirs.

_____ 9. Some people don't think in a(n) ___ way. Their thoughts are governed by emotion, not reason.

_____ 10. There are at least two versions of the joke in which a customer complains that a fly is in his soup. The waiter's ___ is either "That's okay—there's no extra charge" or "Don't worry—he won't drink much."

NOTE: Now check your answers to these questions by turning to page 129. Going over the answers carefully will help you prepare for the next two practices, for which answers are not given.

➢ *Sentence Check 2*

Using the answer lines provided, complete each item below with **two** words from the box. Use each word once.

_____
_____ 1–2. Tony was in ___ of his athletic friend Ben, who seemed to ___ in any contest of strength or speed.

_____
_____ 3–4. The speaker told his high school audience, "I can ___ dozens of cases of adults who mistakenly thought they were ___ from the harm of cocaine. They all eventually lost their jobs and their families."

_____
_____ 5–6. Keith and Sara's matchmaking friends were so sure they'd be ___ that they tried everything to ___ the two into each other's arms.

_____   7–8. The prudent° and ___ thing to do is to ask Michael to return your
_____   sweater before you sneak into his room to ___ it behind his back.

_____   9–10. When I complained to the landlord that the kitchen shelves were so
_____   high they were ___ only by ladder, his ___ was, "So get a ladder!"

➤ *Final Check:* **Our Headstrong Baby**

Here is a final opportunity for you to strengthen your knowledge of the ten words. First read the following selection carefully. Then fill in each blank with a word from the box at the top of the previous page. (Context clues will help you figure out which word goes in which blank.) Use each word once.

Before our child was born, we truly believed we would be (1)_____

from many of the restrictions of our friends who were parents. Being novices° at parenthood, we

were sure a baby and a nicely decorated home could be (2)_____. We

thought we could just explain to the baby in a calm, (3)_____ manner that

certain objects in the house were not to be touched. But now we are parents, and our illusions°

about babies are gone. Now we are in (4)_____ of a tiny infant's amazing

abilities. We've learned that when an adult and a baby disagree, the baby will almost always

(5)_____. We've learned, too, that a child who can't even crawl can

somehow (6)_____ its little body over to an object that attracts it. It took us

a while to admit defeat—we could (7)_____ examples of vases broken and

books chewed into pulp. But we finally gave up and realized it was up to us, not the baby, to avert°

daily destruction. We look at our formerly attractive house now and see that every surface which is

(8)_____ to the baby has been cleared of everything but toys. So now, when

our childless friends laugh at us as we (9)_____ our belongings from the

uppermost shelves of the house, this is our (10)_____: "We'll listen to you

when you have a kid of your own."

Scores	Sentence Check 2 _____%	Final Check _____%

Enter your scores above and in the vocabulary performance chart on the inside back cover of the book.

elapse	infer
evasive	lethal
fluent	obsession
futile	ordeal
harass	persistent

Ten Words in Context

In the space provided, write the letter of the meaning closest to that of each **boldfaced** word. Use the context of the sentences to help you figure out each word's meaning.

1 elapse
(ĭ-lăps′)
-verb

- When I'm busy with work I enjoy, the hours seem to **elapse** quickly.
- Although four years had **elapsed** since I last saw Marian, we talked as if we'd never parted.

__ *Elapse* means   a. to develop.   b. to go back.   c. to go by.

2 evasive
(ĭ-vā′sĭv)
-adjective

- The Rothmans worried that their son was hiding something when he became **evasive** about where he had been and what he'd been doing.
- We didn't want anyone at school to know our father was in the hospital, so we were **evasive** about him, saying only, "He has to be away for a while."

__ *Evasive* means   a. truthful.   b. indefinite.   c. detailed.

3 fluent
(floo′ənt)
-adjective

- To work in a foreign country, it helps to be **fluent** in its language.
- Jenna wanted to hear what was wrong with her car in simple, everyday words. She was not **fluent** in the language of auto mechanics.

__ *Fluent* means   a. able to remember.   b. able to teach.   c. able to express oneself.

4 futile
(fyoot′l)
-adjective

- My best friend is so stubborn that once he has made a decision, it is **futile** to try to change his mind.
- I'm convinced that washing machines eat socks, so it is **futile** to try to find matching pairs in a load of clean laundry.

__ *Futile* means   a. hopeless.   b. easy.   c. useful.

5 harass
(hə-răs′)
-verb

- A few students in the cafeteria like to **harass** everyone else by frequently clinking their silverware and stamping their feet.
- Sometimes it doesn't help to **harass** people about quitting smoking. Bothering them all the time may make them resist quitting.

__ *Harass* means   a. to injure.   b. to annoy.   c. to please.

6 infer
(ĭn-fûr′)
-verb

- The fact that the old man left his fortune to strangers led us to **infer** he was not fond of his children.
- Since you went hiking on Super Bowl Sunday, I **inferred** that you were not a football fan.

__ *Infer* means   a. to conclude.   b. to forget.   c. to conceal.

7 lethal
(lē′thəl)
-adjective

- My father is not alive today because of a **lethal** combination of driving and drinking.
- Jake is so good at karate that his hands are **lethal** weapons. Because he realizes he could kill somebody, he wouldn't use karate lightly.

___ *Lethal* means   a. rare.   b. deadly.   c. hopeful.

8 obsession
(əb-sĕsh′ən)
-noun

- Psychologists help people troubled by **obsessions** to gain control over their thinking, so they are not bothered by the same thoughts over and over.
- Going to garage sales was at first just a hobby. But bargain-hunting has become such an **obsession** that I can't seem to stop going to them.

___ *Obsession* means   a. a helpful habit.   b. a possession.   c. a constant thought.

9 ordeal
(ôr-dēl′)
-noun

- Even if you are in good physical condition, running cross-country is an **ordeal**.
- Hannah came out of the difficult three-hour test, sighed, and said, "What an **ordeal**. I'm worn out."

___ *Ordeal* means   a. a welcome event.   b. a sure success.   c. a difficult challenge.

10 persistent
(pər-sĭs′tənt)
-adjective

- At first Tony wouldn't go out with Lola, but she was **persistent** in asking him. Now they're engaged.
- I am a very **persistent** salesman. I work with customers for as long as it takes for them to buy something.

___ *Persistent* means   a. stubborn.   b. useless.   c. late.

Matching Words with Definitions

Following are definitions of the ten words. Clearly write or print each word next to its definition. The sentences above and on the previous page will help you decide on the meaning of each word.

1. _____   To draw a conclusion from evidence

2. _____   An idea or feeling, often unreasonable, which completely fills someone's mind

3. _____   A very difficult or painful experience

4. _____   Deliberately unclear

5. _____   Useless; unable to succeed

6. _____   Able to cause death; deadly

7. _____   Refusing to quit; stubbornly continuing

8. _____   To pass or slip by (usually said of time)

9. _____   Able to express oneself with skill and ease

10. _____   To constantly irritate or disturb; bother

CAUTION: Do not go any further until you are sure the above answers are correct. Then you can use the definitions to help you in the following practices. Your goal is eventually to know the words well enough so that you don't need to check the definitions at all.

➤ Sentence Check 1

Using the answer line provided, complete each item below with the correct word from the box. Use each word once.

a. **elapse**	b. **evasive**	c. **fluent**	d. **futile**	e. **harass**
f. **infer**	g. **lethal**	h. **obsession**	i. **ordeal**	j. **persistent**

_____ 1. Roger knew a few Chinese phrases, but he was not ___ enough in Chinese to carry on a conversation.

_____ 2. Photographers ___(e)d the movie star, photographing her even on a private beach.

_____ 3. When I'm on a diet, eating pizza becomes an ___ for me.

_____ 4. Reporters tried to pin the president down on his plan to rescue the hostages, but he always gave a(n) ___ answer.

_____ 5. After ten seconds ___, a bell rings, and the game-show host reads the next question.

_____ 6. Selling drugs can be a(n) ___ occupation—there is almost one drug-related murder a day in Philadelphia alone.

_____ 7. Going to the veterinarian is a real ___ for our dog, who begins to shiver in fear at the sight of the vet's office.

_____ 8. It is ___ to try to have a conversation with Manny when a football game is on television because his eyes are glued to the set.

_____ 9. Carlos had to work full-time to support his family, but he still earned his college degree by being ___ in his studies even when he was busy or tired.

_____ 10. It was easy for the teacher to ___ that one of the students had copied the other's paper—both had the same wording in several paragraphs.

NOTE: Now check your answers to these questions by turning to page 130. Going over the answers carefully will help you prepare for the next two practices, for which answers are not given.

➤ Sentence Check 2

Using the answer lines provided, complete each item below with **two** words from the box. Use each word once.

_____
_____ 1–2. Wild mushrooms were an ___ of my aunt, who picked and ate them whenever possible. Unfortunately, her abnormal interest proved ___, for she died after a meal of poisonous creamed mushrooms on toast.

_____
_____ 3–4. The student hesitated and then gave a vague answer. "From your ___ answer," said the teacher, "I ___ that you haven't studied the chapter. In the future, maybe you could put a few minutes of homework on your daily schedule."

_____ 5–6. Five days ___(e)d before the forest fire was put out. It was an especially
_____   difficult ___ for the firefighters, who had to get by on very little sleep.

_____ 7–8. You must be ___ in learning a language if you wish to become ___ in
_____   it.

_____ 9–10. Cats on my street have learned they can safely ___ the dog chained in my
_____   neighbor's yard. And they derive° much pleasure from doing so. The poor
       dog, however, hasn't seemed to learn that it is ___ to threaten the cats.

➤ *Final Check:* **A Narrow Escape**

Here is a final opportunity for you to strengthen your knowledge of the ten words. First read the following selection carefully. Then fill in each blank with a word from the box at the top of the previous page. (Context clues will help you figure out which word goes in which blank.) Use each word once.

    "They're going to kidnap and kill us. They're going to kidnap and kill us." The gruesome° thought had become an (1)_____—I could think of nothing else. When Craig and I had hopped into the truck to hitch a ride toward Frankfurt, Germany, the two truck drivers were very friendly. Although we were not (2)_____ in their language—we couldn't even figure out what language they were speaking, but we knew it wasn't German—they spoke a little English. So we could (3)_____ from their words and motions that they would take us to Frankfurt after they delivered a package. But they drove around for such a long time that we began to doubt that they really were making a delivery. As the hours (4)_____(e)d, we became worried. Our worry turned to fear as we realized the men were arguing, and it seemed to be about *us*. Occasionally the driver would ask us a question, like "Your parents rich Americans?" or "You their only child?" Craig and I began asking to be let out so we could get another ride. The men apologized for the delay and were (5)_____ in repeating their promise to get us to Frankfurt "very soon." But they became more and more (6)_____ about exactly when "very soon" would be. Although it was dark and we had no idea where we were, we decided we had to get out of that truck, so we demanded to be dropped off. Instead, they drove to an empty warehouse in the middle of nowhere. The driver showed us a long knife and said, "You give us your parents' address." That's when I knew we were being kidnapped. With the truck finally stopped, I grabbed the door handle and tried to get out. But my efforts were (7)_____; the door was locked. Knowing the driver had a (8)_____ weapon scared me badly, but trying to sound braver than I felt, I shouted, "Let us out NOW!" Craig joined me in shouting at the men. Suddenly they began arguing in their own language again; the second man seemed to be (9)_____ing the driver to do something. Finally the driver threw up his hands in disgust. The second man unlocked the door, opened it, and shouted "YOU OUT NOW." He didn't have to say it twice. We flew out of that truck and eventually found our way to a town. We could hardly believe that our (10)_____ was over and we were safe.

Scores	Sentence Check 2 _____%	Final Check _____%	

Enter your scores above and in the vocabulary performance chart on the inside back cover of the book.

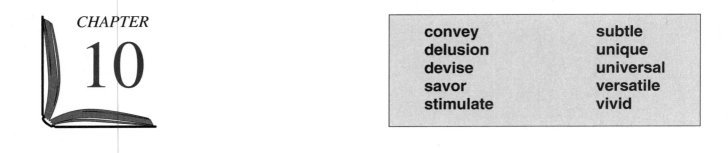

convey	subtle
delusion	unique
devise	universal
savor	versatile
stimulate	vivid

Ten Words in Context

In the space provided, write the letter of the meaning closest to that of each **boldfaced** word. Use the context of the sentences to help you figure out each word's meaning.

1 **convey**
(kən-vā′)
-*verb*

- Using sign language, chimpanzees can **convey** such ideas as "Candy sweet" and "Give me hug."
- On my parents' twenty-fifth wedding anniversary, I sent a telegram to **convey** my congratulations and love.

___ *Convey* means 　　a. to think of. 　　b. to prevent. 　　c. to communicate.

2 **delusion**
(dĭ-loo′zhən)
-*noun*

- Alex clings to the **delusion** of being in total control even when drunk. In reality, he then lacks both judgment and muscle control.
- Quincy holds the **delusion** that money is everything. Sadly, in seeking financial success, he neglects what is truly important, such as family and friends.

___ *Delusion* means 　　a. a pleasure. 　　b. a misbelief. 　　c. an action.

3 **devise**
(dĭ-vīz′)
-*verb*

- In the 1880s an American woman **devised** a machine that sprayed dinnerware with hot, soapy water—the first automatic dishwasher.
- The police had **devised** a plan to catch the thief, but he escaped through the freight elevator.

___ *Devise* means 　　a. to create. 　　b. to forget. 　　c. to carry.

4 **savor**
(sā′vər)
-*verb*

- Katie **savored** the candy bar, eating it bit by bit so that the pleasure would last as long as possible.
- Given a rare chance to enjoy the beach, I **savored** every moment in the warm sun.

___ *Savor* means 　　a. to save for later. 　　b. to enjoy. 　　c. to ignore.

5 **stimulate**
(stĭm′yə-lāt′)
-*verb*

- The teacher hoped to **stimulate** her students' interest in reading by choosing books that related to their own lives.
- I tried to **stimulate** my sick rabbit's appetite by offering him choice bits of carrots and celery.

___ *Stimulate* means 　　a. to make active. 　　b. to recognize. 　　c. to discourage.

6 **subtle**
(sŭt′l)
-*adjective*

- Animal actors are trained to respond to human signals too **subtle** to be noticed by the audience.
- Although Yasmin was born in Alabama, she has lived in New York for many years. As a result, her Southern accent is so **subtle** that some of her friends don't even notice it.

___ *Subtle* means 　　a. obvious. 　　b. peaceful. 　　c. slight.

7 unique
(yōō-nēk′)
-adjective

- Any live musical performance is **unique**—the music will never again be played in exactly the same way.
- My talents are **unique** in my family. For example, I'm the only one who can whistle through my nose.

___ *Unique* means   a. active.   b. hardly noticeable.   c. one of a kind.

8 universal
(yōō′nə-vûr′səl)
-adjective

- The United Nations was founded to advance **universal** freedom and peace.
- The film had **universal** success—it was a hit in all parts of the United States and in other countries as well.

___ *Universal* means   a. limited.   b. throughout the world.   c. throughout time.

9 versatile
(vûr′sə-təl)
-adjective

- Our new computer is **versatile**. It can balance the family checkbook, do word processing, keep tax records, and play against me in chess.
- Edie is the most **versatile** person I know: she paints, sings, does gymnastics, and is a math whiz.

___ *Versatile* means   a. having many abilities.   b. boring.   c. out of control.

10 vivid
(vĭv′ĭd)
-adjective

- To make the living room bright and dramatic, we decorated it in **vivid** shades of red.
- At funerals, most people wear black or dark gray clothing with little or no **vivid** color.

___ *Vivid* means   a. dull.   b. bright.   c. pale.

Matching Words with Definitions

Following are definitions of the ten words. Clearly write or print each word next to its definition. The sentences above and on the previous page will help you decide on the meaning of each word.

1. _____   Unlike any other; one of a kind

2. _____   To invent; think up; create

3. _____   Bright; brightly colored; striking

4. _____   Hardly noticeable; not obvious

5. _____   To communicate; make known

6. _____   To cause to become active or more active; arouse

7. _____   Worldwide; widespread

8. _____   To taste or smell with pleasure; to appreciate fully

9. _____   A false opinion or belief

10. _____   Able to do many things or serve many purposes well

CAUTION: Do not go any further until you are sure the above answers are correct. Then you can use the definitions to help you in the following practices. Your goal is eventually to know the words well enough so that you don't need to check the definitions at all.

➤ *Sentence Check 1*

Using the answer line provided, complete each item below with the correct word from the box. Use each word once.

a. convey	b. delusion	c. devise	d. savor	e. stimulate
f. subtle	g. unique	h. universal	i. versatile	j. vivid

_____ 1. The chimp ___(e)d a way of reaching the banana that hung from the ceiling. She piled one box on top of another and climbed up.

_____ 2. The "terrible twos" is a ___ stage of childhood. In every culture, children start demanding independence at about this age.

_____ 3. Breathing deeply, I ___(e)d my favorite summer smell—freshly-cut grass.

_____ 4. Pam's eyes blinked a ___ message that only her husband saw: "I think we should get ready to leave before it gets any later."

_____ 5. The painting, with its bright stripes of shocking pink, green, and yellow, was so ___ that it glowed even in dim light.

_____ 6. Even if Mr. Pierce sang his lecture while dancing on his desk, he couldn't ___ my interest in geology. To me, it's the most boring of subjects.

_____ 7. When Edward saw the Grand Canyon, he made no attempt to describe it on a postcard. He felt that the glories of this natural wonder were too amazing to ___ in words.

_____ 8. "I thought she loved me, but it was just a ___," said Lawrence. "She was just a good friend."

_____ 9. This Egyptian bracelet is ___ since no other bracelet in the world is made with the same combination of gems and precious metals.

_____ 10. From a child's point of view, a simple brown box is very ___. It can be a dollhouse, a bucket, a desk, or even a funny hat.

NOTE: Now check your answers to these questions by turning to page 130. Going over the answers carefully will help you prepare for the next two practices, for which answers are not given.

➤ *Sentence Check 2*

Using the answer lines provided, complete each item below with **two** words from the box. Use each word once.

_____
_____ 1–2. When Jill applies for a job, it will be to her advantage to ___ to interviewers just how ___ she is. Employers will welcome her many different skills.

_____
_____ 3–4. I ___ the time I have alone with my brother, who is unlike anyone else. He has a ___ way of looking at things.

_____ 5–6. I wish someone would ___ a way to ___ children's appetites so they
_____   will feel hungry for something besides pizza and peanut butter.

_____ 7–8. Rosa enjoys wearing ___ colors, like red and purple, but I prefer more
_____   ___ shades, such as pale pinks and blues.

_____ 9–10. Denny truly believes that ___ peace will occur during his lifetime.
_____   However, I think that the possibility of world harmony is a ___.

➤ _Final Check:_ The Power of Advertising

Here is a final opportunity for you to strengthen your knowledge of the ten words. First read the following selection carefully. Then fill in each blank with a word from the box at the top of the previous page. (Context clues will help you figure out which word goes in which blank.) Use each word once.

I am convinced that advertising agencies could sell people last week's garbage. They make everything sound good. Using evasive° language, advertisers make such vague but impressive statements as "Professionals recommend our skin creams." (The careful consumer will ask, "Professionals in what field?") The agencies are also skilled at using richly appealing images. For example, newspaper ads never sell "brightly colored towels." Instead they sell "petal-soft bath sheets in a variety of (1)_____ rainbow colors." Perfumes in ads don't make you "smell good"; they "invite you to please that special man in your life with this (2)_____ yet unmistakable odor of tea roses." Food ads (3)_____ your appetite by offering "a sauce carefully blended to produce an unforgettable taste that you and your guests will (4)_____." Clothing ads (5)_____ the idea that if you wear a particular suit or dress, you will be classier than the next person. Other ads, such as those for computers, tell you how (6)_____ their products will make you, suggesting that they will give you more skills than others have. Advertisements must have (7)_____ appeal to attract millions of people. Yet they must also persuade all those people to accept the (8)_____ that they will be (9)_____ if they buy a particular product. Yes, I bet that if an advertising agency wanted to sell last week's garbage, it would simply (10)_____ an ad saying, "Nowhere else can you find a gift with so powerful an aroma that it overflows with bittersweet memories of yesterday, yet hints that it will grow stronger with each passing day."

| _Scores_ | Sentence Check 2 _____% | Final Check _____% |

Enter your scores above and in the vocabulary performance chart on the inside back cover of the book.

UNIT TWO: Review

The box at the right lists twenty-five words from Unit Two. Using the clues at the bottom of the page, fill in these words to complete the puzzle that follows.

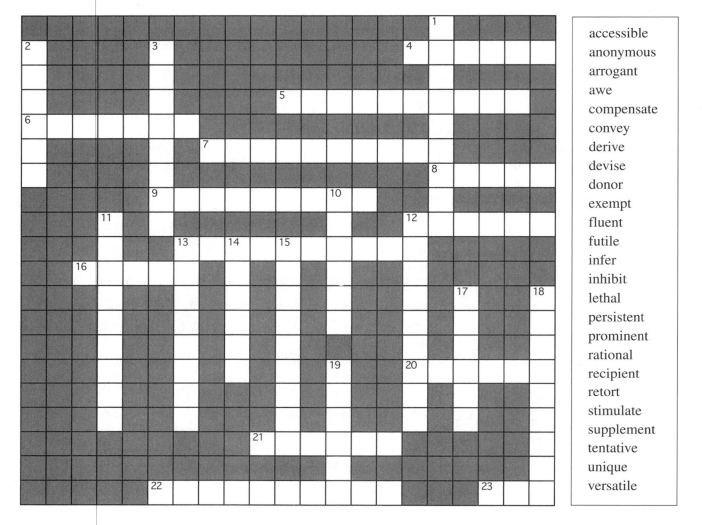

accessible
anonymous
arrogant
awe
compensate
convey
derive
devise
donor
exempt
fluent
futile
infer
inhibit
lethal
persistent
prominent
rational
recipient
retort
stimulate
supplement
tentative
unique
versatile

ACROSS

4. Able to cause death; deadly
5. To make suitable payment to; pay; repay
6. To hold back; prevent
7. To add to, especially to make up for a lack
8. To draw a conclusion from evidence
9. Created or given by an unknown or unidentified person
12. A sharp or clever reply
13. Easily reached or entered
16. A person who gives or contributes
20. Free from some unpleasant duty or situation
21. To receive from a source; get
22. Refusing to quit; stubbornly continuing
23. Great respect mixed with wonder and fear

DOWN

1. Able to do many things well
2. To invent; think up; create
3. Reasonable; logical
10. Unlike any other; one of a kind
11. Very noticeable; obvious
12. A person who receives
13. Filled with self-importance; overly proud and vain
14. To communicate; make known
15. To cause to become active or more active; arouse
17. Able to speak a language with skill and ease
18. Not definite; not final
19. Useless; unable to succeed

UNIT TWO: Test 1

PART A
Choose the word that best completes each item and write it in the space provided.

_____ 1. I used a fishing pole to ___ my hat from the duck pond.

    a. savor   b. retrieve   c. infer   d. stimulate

_____ 2. My sister's ___ about snakes is so strong she actually faints if she sees one.

    a. phobia   b. retort   c. diversity   d. donor

_____ 3. The air escaping from the balloon ___ it across the table and into the punch bowl.

    a. propelled   b. devised   c. inferred   d. surpassed

_____ 4. I knew Jackie would do well in the pole vault, but her wonderful performance ___ even my expectations.

    a. devised   b. bestowed   c. surpassed   d. conveyed

_____ 5. Lisa, who is unusually short, had her kitchen built with cabinets low enough to be ___ to her.

    a. subtle   b. prudent   c. accessible   d. vivid

_____ 6. After denting his parents' car, Victor let several months ___ before he asked to borrow the car again.

    a. supplement   b. prevail   c. devise   d. elapse

_____ 7. Using only gestures, Tina managed to ___ to Jerry the message that she would meet him at the Student Center at two o'clock.

    a. surpass   b. savor   c. cite   d. convey

_____ 8. We usually don't think about the fact that our books, newspapers, and wooden furniture are all ___ from trees.

    a. cited   b. derived   c. verified   d. compensated

_____ 9. Since kids sometimes call in orders to pizza parlors as a joke, some pizza clerks now call back to ___ that each order is genuine.

    a. elapse   b. verify   c. stimulate   d. bestow

_____ 10. Rita turned her ___ of being lost in the desert into good fortune by selling the story to a movie studio.

    a. ordeal   b. diversity   c. retort   d. recipient

(Continues on next page)

PART B

On the answer line, write the letter of the choice that best completes each item.

_____ 11. My aunt's new kitchen appliance is truly **versatile**. It
    a. takes up a great deal of space.   b. squeezes oranges.
    c. makes toast, brews coffee, and fries bacon.   d. cost more than $500.

_____ 12. One way to **inhibit** the growth of a plant or bush is to
    a. water it whenever it begins to look dry.   b. give it lots of plant food.
    c. trim it daily.   d. talk to it.

_____ 13. The mosquito was so **persistent** that it
    a. wouldn't stop buzzing around my head.   b. couldn't be found.
    c. weaved back and forth as it flew.   d. flew away immediately.

_____ 14. Lydia was **apprehensive** about going to an Indian restaurant because she
    a. enjoyed all Indian foods.   b. was afraid the food might be too spicy.
    c. was curious about new foods.   d. didn't have to work that day.

_____ 15. One quality shared by all **anonymous** writers is that they
    a. are very well-paid.   b. never get their work published.
    c. do not tell the truth.   d. do not want their identities known.

_____ 16. "Be careful of that vase—it's **unique**," my grandmother said. She meant that the vase was
    a. fragile.   b. very expensive.
    c. the only one of its kind.   d. from another country.

_____ 17. I **inferred** that Julia and Roberto had had a fight when I
    a. saw them fighting.
    b. heard an untrue rumor that they had fought.
    c. saw they were holding hands.
    d. saw her pass right by him without speaking to him.

_____ 18. The change in Eleanor's hair color is so **subtle** that
    a. friends keep saying, "Holy cow, Eleanor—what did you do to your hair?"
    b. everyone comments on how good the new color looks.
    c. only her best friend noticed it.
    d. no one mentions it, for fear of embarrassing her by telling her how ugly it is.

_____ 19. I knew my girlfriend and I were **compatible** when
    a. we discovered we both love horror movies and smelly cheese.
    b. she groaned at my choices of novels and CDs.
    c. we learned we were both born in the summer.
    d. she refused to go to football games with me.

_____ 20. Which of the following famous scenes from Shakespeare's plays demonstrates an **obsession**?
    a. The fairy Puck turns one character into a donkey (in _A Midsummer Night's Dream_).
    b. Lady Macbeth washes her hands again and again to try to remove imaginary blood (in _Macbeth_).
    c. The two young lovers first meet at a ball given by Juliet's family (in _Romeo and Juliet_).
    d. The king decides to divide his kingdom among his three daughters (in _King Lear_).

Score (Number correct) _____ x 5 = _____ %

Enter your score above and in the vocabulary performance chart on the inside back cover of the book.

UNIT TWO: Test 2

PART A
Complete each item with a word from the box. Use each word once.

a. **arrogant**	b. **awe**	c. **compensate**	d. **delusion**	e. **diversity**
f. **lethal**	g. **prudent**	h. **rational**	i. **retort**	j. **savor**
k. **supplement**	l. **tentative**	m. **universal**		

_____ 1. It's dangerous to mix chlorine bleach and other household cleaners. The combination can produce ___ fumes.

_____ 2. Knowing the ice cream would be his last before beginning his diet, Jon took time to ___ every rich spoonful.

_____ 3. I can't stand that ___ movie critic. He always speaks as if his reviews came directly from God.

_____ 4. I hung my dress outside the dry-cleaning shop when the owner refused to ___ me for ruining it by running the colors together.

_____ 5. The German and American children didn't mind that they couldn't speak the same language. They all knew the ___ language of play.

_____ 6. After running out of gas on the way to the hospital for an emergency, I decided it was ___ to keep the tank full at all times.

_____ 7. The mugger's victim made a(n) ___ identification of her attacker from a photo. However, she said she would have to see him in person to be sure.

_____ 8. The young mother was still giving her toddler only milk. The doctor explained that it was time for her to ___ the child's diet with solid food.

_____ 9. I like our women's group because of its ___. Among the black, Hispanic and white members are grandmothers, young mothers, and young single women.

_____ 10. It's thrilling to watch Allen Iverson play basketball. His athletic ability fills me with ___.

_____ 11. Rosa is overly ___ about her love life. She lists a guy's good and bad qualities before deciding if she'll date him again.

_____ 12. When someone is rude to me, I'd love to make a clever ___, but a snappy comeback never occurs to me until hours later.

_____ 13. The town's belief that the company was loyal to its workers proved to be a ___. The company laid everyone off and moved the plant to a state with cheaper labor.

(Continues on next page)

PART B
Write **C** if the italicized word is used **correctly**. Write **I** if the word is used **incorrectly**.

_____ 14. After being the *recipient* of seven speeding tickets in one month, Marylee lost her license.

_____ 15. At some health clinics, people with little income are *exempt* from all fees.

_____ 16. Sally always dresses in *vivid* colors, such as pastel pink or light grey.

_____ 17. It's easy to find Dwight's house because of the *prominent* display of pink flamingos on the lawn.

_____ 18. Owen bragged that when he got rich, he would buy his mother the most *moderate* diamond necklace in town. He wanted her to have the best.

_____ 19. I'm a little angry at our neighbor Henry. I told him to take just a few tomatoes from our garden, not to *bestow* all the ripe ones.

_____ 20. After Judy's wonderful performance in the play, friends rushed backstage to *harass* her with flowers and praise.

_____ 21. Lynn has repeatedly asked Brian exactly what he does for a living, but she always gets an *evasive* answer like "I work downtown."

_____ 22. My overactive young nephew takes medicine to *stimulate* his tendency to race around the house and throw things.

_____ 23. Tony was disappointed when he *prevailed* in the student council election. Maybe he'll do better next year.

_____ 24. When my sister doubled over with sudden, *acute* pain, we suspected that her appendix had become infected.

_____ 25. To make my point that school can be as stressful as a full-time job, I *cited* the pressures of being a student.

Score   (Number correct) _____ x 4 = _____ %

Enter your score above and in the vocabulary performance chart on the inside back cover of the book.

UNIT TWO: *Test 3*

PART A: Synonyms
In the space provided, write the letter of the choice that is most nearly the **same** in meaning as the **boldfaced** word.

_____ 1. **compensate**   **a)** pay   **b)** pass   **c)** prove   **d)** decide

_____ 2. **retort**   **a)** add to   **b)** know   **c)** reply   **d)** get back

_____ 3. **awe**   **a)** hate   **b)** respect   **c)** regret   **d)** confusion

_____ 4. **lethal**   **a)** extreme   **b)** modest   **c)** wise   **d)** deadly

_____ 5. **fluent**   **a)** smooth-speaking   **b)** full   **c)** not obvious   **d)** reachable

_____ 6. **savor**   **a)** win   **b)** answer   **c)** enjoy   **d)** hide

_____ 7. **elapse**   **a)** please   **b)** pass   **c)** outdo   **d)** gather

_____ 8. **retrieve**   **a)** send   **b)** walk around   **c)** think up   **d)** get back

_____ 9. **verify**   **a)** prove   **b)** add to   **c)** repay   **d)** contradict

_____ 10. **infer**   **a)** reply   **b)** mention   **c)** conclude   **d)** do better than

_____ 11. **accessible**   **a)** having great variety   **b)** logical   **c)** not obvious   **d)** reachable

_____ 12. **obsession**   **a)** pay   **b)** painful experience   **c)** variety   **d)** idea of extreme concern

_____ 13. **exempt**   **a)** wise   **b)** lively   **c)** excused   **d)** fearful

_____ 14. **surpass**   **a)** support   **b)** outdo   **c)** lose   **d)** invent

_____ 15. **cite**   **a)** mention   **b)** locate   **c)** pass   **d)** delay

_____ 16. **apprehensive**   **a)** unclear   **b)** able to do many things well   **c)** deadly   **d)** fearful

_____ 17. **devise**   **a)** create   **b)** receive   **c)** prevent   **d)** repay

_____ 18. **supplement**   **a)** win out   **b)** owe   **c)** add to   **d)** provide the moving force

_____ 19. **convey**   **a)** invent   **b)** communicate   **c)** cause to grow   **d)** test

_____ 20. **versatile**   **a)** having many skills   **b)** average   **c)** musical   **d)** not final

_____ 21. **conceive**   **a)** imagine   **b)** forget   **c)** apply   **d)** promote

_____ 22. **phobia**   **a)** confusion   **b)** fear   **c)** memory   **d)** nightmare

_____ 23. **propel**   **a)** chase   **b)** win out   **c)** move forward   **d)** fly

_____ 24. **delusion**   **a)** truth   **b)** bad dream   **c)** clever trick   **d)** false belief

_____ 25. **universal**   **a)** worldwide   **b)** unfinished   **c)** together   **d)** not obvious

(Continues on next page)

PART B: Antonyms
In the space provided, write the letter of the choice that is most nearly the **opposite** in meaning to the **boldfaced** word.

_____ 26. **prevail**   **a)** discourage   **b)** give   **c)** hide   **d)** lose

_____ 27. **arrogant**   **a)** modest   **b)** helpful   **c)** relaxed   **d)** stubborn

_____ 28. **rational**   **a)** illegal   **b)** unreasonable   **c)** unreliable   **d)** mild

_____ 29. **anonymous**   **a)** unknown   **b)** common   **c)** identified   **d)** dull

_____ 30. **donor**   **a)** boss   **b)** organizer   **c)** newcomer   **d)** one who receives

_____ 31. **prominent**   **a)** bright   **b)** misleading   **c)** unnoticeable   **d)** unwise

_____ 32. **diversity**   **a)** disrespect   **b)** sameness   **c)** difficulty   **d)** question

_____ 33. **prudent**   **a)** unwise   **b)** unknown   **c)** shy   **d)** straightforward

_____ 34. **moderate**   **a)** conceited   **b)** old   **c)** extreme   **d)** courageous

_____ 35. **derive**   **a)** give   **b)** stand still   **c)** win   **d)** discourage

_____ 36. **acute**   **a)** unreasonable   **b)** mild   **c)** obvious   **d)** definite

_____ 37. **persistent**   **a)** not well-known   **b)** dull   **c)** illogical   **d)** giving up

_____ 38. **recipient**   **a)** employee   **b)** one who gives   **c)** one who asks   **d)** owner

_____ 39. **evasive**   **a)** light   **b)** common   **c)** straightforward   **d)** healthy

_____ 40. **subtle**   **a)** young   **b)** humble   **c)** continuing   **d)** obvious

_____ 41. **vivid**   **a)** lively   **b)** dull   **c)** late   **d)** required

_____ 42. **ordeal**   **a)** pleasant experience   **b)** sale   **c)** variety   **d)** question

_____ 43. **tentative**   **a)** fearful   **b)** definite   **c)** misleading   **d)** illogical

_____ 44. **stimulate**   **a)** enjoy   **b)** hint at   **c)** discourage   **d)** disappear

_____ 45. **unique**   **a)** rare   **b)** famous   **c)** common   **d)** unknown

_____ 46. **compatible**   **a)** mismatched   **b)** sunken   **c)** clear   **d)** reversible

_____ 47. **inhibit**   **a)** leave   **b)** encourage   **c)** win   **d)** declare

_____ 48. **bestow**   **a)** pardon   **b)** find   **c)** destroy   **d)** receive

_____ 49. **harass**   **a)** admire   **b)** release   **c)** comfort   **d)** delay

_____ 50. **futile**   **a)** lively   **b)** useful   **c)** past   **d)** dull

Score   (Number correct) _____ x 2 = _____%

Enter your score above and in the vocabulary performance chart on the inside back cover of the book.

UNIT TWO: Test 4

Each item below starts with a pair of words in CAPITAL LETTERS. For each item, figure out the relationship between these two words. Then decide which of the choices (*a*, *b*, *c*, or *d*) expresses a similar relationship. Write the letter of your choice on the answer line.

_____ 1. COMPENSATE : PAYCHECK ::

    a. recognize : sale   b. reward : tax

    c. envelope : letter   d. punish : fine

_____ 2. CONCEIVE : IDEA ::

    a. melt : mountain   b. paint : picture

    c. build : hole   d. drip : ship

_____ 3. DIVERSITY : VARIETY ::

    a. place : location   b. similarity : twins

    c. cause : effect   d. weight : height

_____ 4. VERIFY : DISPROVE ::

    a. surrender : resist   b. select : know

    c. lose : compete   d. explore : find

_____ 5. ACUTE : MILD ::

    a. delicious : taste   b. new : expensive

    c. tall : height   d. violent : peaceful

_____ 6. DONOR : GIVE ::

    a. player : stay   b. child : remain

    c. thief : steal   d. musician : lead

_____ 7. ANONYMOUS : NAME ::

    a. funny : humor   b. strong : health

    c. tall : height   d. poor : money

_____ 8. PRUDENT : WISE ::

    a. vain : modest   b. pretty : attractive

    c. strong : weights   d. serious : joking

_____ 9. ACCESSIBLE : ENTER ::

    a. invisible : see   b. lovable : hate

    c. impossible : do   d. preventable : avoid

_____ 10. AWE : RESPECT ::

    a. adoration : love   b. anger : affection

    c. attraction : disgust   d. amusement : sorrow

(Continues on next page)

_____ 11. PROPEL : BASEBALL ::

    a. float : rock   b. hang : laundry
    c. dig : deep   d. shake : television

_____ 12. RETRIEVE : GET BACK ::

    a. remove : keep   b. reward : punish
    c. recall : remember   d. receive : repeat

_____ 13. LETHAL : HEALTHFUL ::

    a. close : near   b. useful : helpful
    c. kind : mean   d. blue : navy

_____ 14. FLUENT : SPEAKER ::

    a. warm : snow   b. graceful : dancer
    c. long : cure   d. green : skies

_____ 15. FUTILE : USEFUL ::

    a. easy : simple   b. slight : great
    c. fatal : deadly   d. red : scarlet

_____ 16. ORDEAL : TERM PAPER ::

    a. conflict : conclusion   b. trial : verdict
    c. injury : full recovery   d. challenge : final exam

_____ 17. DELUSION : MIND ::

    a. disease : body   b. heart : lungs
    c. thorn : daisy   d. nutrition : health

_____ 18. DEVISE : INVENTION ::

    a. play : workplace   b. write : essay
    c. read : glasses   d. carve : skill

_____ 19. SUBTLE : OBVIOUS ::

    a. bright : light   b. written : pencil
    c. factual : realistic   d. hinted at: stated

_____ 20. UNIQUE : ONE ::

    a. multiple : many   b. three : six
    c. two : three   d. numerous : few

Score (Number correct) _____ x 5 = _____%	

Enter your score above and in the vocabulary performance chart on the inside back cover of the book.

Unit Three

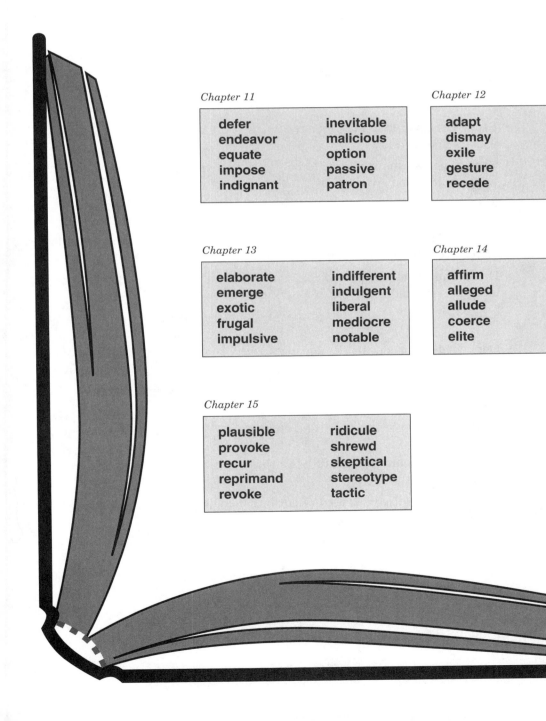

Chapter 11

defer	inevitable
endeavor	malicious
equate	option
impose	passive
indignant	patron

Chapter 12

adapt	reciprocate
dismay	refute
exile	retain
gesture	revert
recede	ritual

Chapter 13

elaborate	indifferent
emerge	indulgent
exotic	liberal
frugal	mediocre
impulsive	notable

Chapter 14

affirm	essence
alleged	immunity
allude	impair
coerce	query
elite	sadistic

Chapter 15

plausible	ridicule
provoke	shrewd
recur	skeptical
reprimand	stereotype
revoke	tactic

defer	inevitable
endeavor	malicious
equate	option
impose	passive
indignant	patron

Ten Words in Context

In the space provided, write the letter of the meaning closest to that of each **boldfaced** word. Use the context of the sentences to help you figure out each word's meaning.

1 defer
(dĭ-fûr′)
-*verb*

- The children showed great respect for their grandmother and **deferred** to her every wish.
- When it comes to fixing cars, I **defer** to my brother's judgment. He knows much more about auto mechanics than I do.

___ *Defer* means   a. to object.   b. to give in.   c. to avoid.

2 endeavor
(ĕn-dĕv′ər)
-*verb*

- Becky **endeavored** to raise money for Christmas presents by selling candy and cookies door to door.
- Your company would be wise to hire Jesse. He will **endeavor** to do his best at whatever jobs you give him.

___ *Endeavor* means   a. to try.   b. to pretend.   c. to step aside.

3 equate
(ĭ-kwāt′)
-*verb*

- It would be a mistake to **equate** the two teams just because they both have perfect records. One team has played much stronger opponents.
- Don't **equate** all homework assignments with busywork. Homework can increase one's understanding of a subject.

___ *Equate* means   a. to exchange.   b. to consider to be the same.   c. to enjoy.

4 impose
(ĭm-pōz′)
-*verb*

- Our neighbor pounded on our door as we were sitting down to eat. "I'm sorry to **impose** on you during dinner," he said, "but I need to borrow a fire extinguisher."
- Roy is always asking favors, yet people never seem to notice how much he **imposes** on them.

___ *Impose* means   a. to selfishly bother.   b. to improve.   c. to spy.

5 indignant
(ĭn-dĭg′nənt)
-*adjective*

- My mother becomes **indignant** when she sees parents treat their children with disrespect.
- When she was falsely accused of stealing the gold chain, the student became very **indignant**.

___ *Indignant* means   a. angry.   b. patient.   c. amused.

6 inevitable
(ĭn-ĕv′ĭ-tə-bəl)
-*adjective*

- I am such a chocoholic that if you put a brownie in front of me, it is **inevitable** that I will eat it.
- We try so hard to look and stay young, but aging is **inevitable**.

___ *Inevitable* means   a. unlikely.   b. surprising.   c. certain.

7 malicious
(mă-lĭsh′əs)
-adjective

- Bullies are **malicious**—they take pleasure in hurting others.
- Rachel loves **malicious** gossip. The more spiteful it is, the more she likes it, and the more likely she is to repeat it.

__ *Malicious* means   a. mean.   b. ambitious.   c. common.

8 option
(ŏp′shən)
-noun

- When the mugger said to me, "Give me your wallet or I'll kill you," I didn't like either **option**.
- Harry thinks a multiple-choice test allows him to choose more than one **option**.

__ *Option* means   a. an opinion.   b. an advantage.   c. a choice.

9 passive
(păs′ĭv)
-adjective

- Taylor is very **passive**. He waits for things to happen instead of making them happen.
- Students learn more when they take part in class discussions instead of simply being **passive** listeners.

__ *Passive* means   a. insincere.   b. inactive.   c. flexible.

10 patron
(pā′trən)
-noun

- The punk-rock star was a good **patron** of the beauty shop. She came in at least once a week to change her hair color.
- Many of the diner's **patrons** were stagehands who worked at the theater across the street.

__ *Patron* means   a. an advertiser.   b. an owner.   c. a customer.

Matching Words with Definitions

Following are definitions of the ten words. Clearly write or print each word next to its definition. The sentences above and on the previous page will help you decide on the meaning of each word.

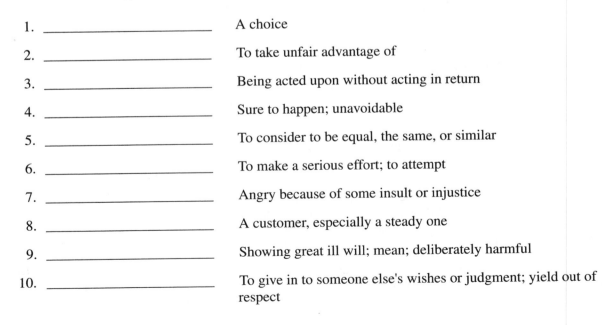

1. _____   A choice

2. _____   To take unfair advantage of

3. _____   Being acted upon without acting in return

4. _____   Sure to happen; unavoidable

5. _____   To consider to be equal, the same, or similar

6. _____   To make a serious effort; to attempt

7. _____   Angry because of some insult or injustice

8. _____   A customer, especially a steady one

9. _____   Showing great ill will; mean; deliberately harmful

10. _____   To give in to someone else's wishes or judgment; yield out of respect

CAUTION: Do not go any further until you are sure the above answers are correct. Then you can use the definitions to help you in the following practices. Your goal is eventually to know the words well enough so that you don't need to check the definitions at all.

➤ *Sentence Check 1*

Using the answer line provided, complete each item below with the correct word from the box. Use each word once.

a. defer	b. endeavor	c. equate	d. impose	e. indignant
f. inevitable	g. malicious	h. option	i. passive	j. patron

_____*f*_____ 1. When rats are crowded together, it's ___ they will fight with each other.

_____*options*_____ 2. I have only two ___s at work: I can do what my boss asks, or I can be fired.

_____*equate*_____ 3. In our society, we too often ___ happiness with money.

_____ 4. Mort isn't a(n) ___ football fan. He actively participates by jumping out of his seat and yelling until he's hoarse.

_____*J*_____ 5. I was the store's most loyal ___ until new management raised the prices, and then I started shopping elsewhere.

_____*G*_____ 6. Heidi is so ___ that she makes up lies to ruin other people's reputations.

_____*D*_____ 7. "I don't want to ___ on you," Scott said, "but if you're going to the post office, would you get me some stamps?"

_____ 8. When his wife accused him of never helping around the house, Mac was _*e*_. Hadn't he just built a deck off the kitchen?

_____*A*_____ 9. Our instructor doesn't expect us to ___ to his opinions just because he's the teacher; he wants us to think for ourselves.

_____*B*_____ 10. Many climbers who have ___(e)d to reach the top of Mount Everest have died on the way.

NOTE: Now check your answers to these questions by turning to page 130. Going over the answers carefully will help you prepare for the next two practices, for which answers are not given.

➤ *Sentence Check 2*

Using the answer lines provided, complete each item below with **two** words from the box. Use each word once.

_____
_____ 1–2. _*e*_ that the boys had thrown rocks at the monkeys and yelled at them, the zookeeper said, "Don't _*C*_ being an animal with having no feelings."

_____
_____ 3–4. Rita, a(n) _*J*_ of Angelo's restaurant for several years, has _*B*_(e)d without success to copy Angelo's delicious spaghetti sauce. Now she has given up. "I've learned it is futile° even to try," she says.

_____
_____ 5–6. "If you remain so _*i*_ that you don't object when Jean takes advantage of you, she'll just _*D*_ on you more and more," my friend warned.

_____   7–8. Since Sam's family is so poor, it seems _F_ he'll work full-time as soon
_____   as he finishes high school. He won't have the _h_ of going to college
                               right away. However, he plans to be prudent° in handling the money
                               he'll earn and then enroll in college in a couple of years.

_____   9–10. Jerome is so _g_ that he goes out of his way to hurt anyone who won't
_____   _A_ to his wishes. I really dislike people who are that mean and self-
                                centered.

➤ *Final Check:* **Waiter**

Here is a final opportunity for you to strengthen your knowledge of the ten words. First read the following
selection carefully. Then fill in each blank with a word from the box at the top of the previous page.
(Context clues will help you figure out which word goes in which blank.) Use each word once.

The loud voice of the young man at the next table startled me. He was (1)_____ _e_ _____

about some undeserved criticism the waiter had received. He said to the waiter, "Why did you just

stand there and let that woman denounce° you like that without sticking up for yourself? You were

like a(n) (2)_____ _passive_ _____ little child."

"I beg your pardon, sir," the waiter answered. "That woman is a(n) (3)_____ _patron_ _____

of this restaurant. I (4)_____ _B_ _____ to treat our customers with respect."

"Even those who (5)_____ _D_ _____ on you by being as demanding as that woman

was? Even those who think they're better than you because you're waiting on them?"

"You seem to (6)_____ _c equate_ _____ my polite manner with weakness," the waiter

answered. "I don't like rude customers, but they're part of a waiter's territory. Standing up publicly

to the woman may seem like a smart move to you, but it would have made two things

(7)_____ _F_ _____: an ugly scene and the loss of my job."

"But you have no (8)_____ _h_ _____," the customer insisted. "You can't let people

step on you, ever—especially when they're being (9)_____ _g_ _____, giving you a hard

time for no good reason."

"You're giving me just as hard a time as that woman did," was the waiter's retort°. "Why

should I (10) _____ _A_ _____ to your opinion and not hers?"

| *Scores* | Sentence Check 2 _____ % | Final Check _____ % |

Enter your scores above and in the vocabulary performance chart on the inside back cover of the book.

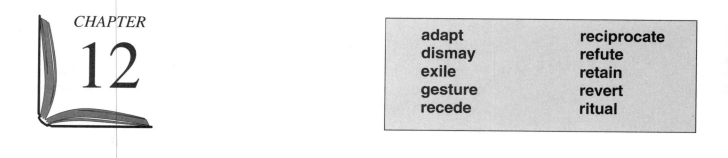

adapt	reciprocate
dismay	refute
exile	retain
gesture	revert
recede	ritual

Ten Words in Context

In the space provided, write the letter of the meaning closest to that of each **boldfaced** word. Use the context of the sentences to help you figure out each word's meaning.

1 adapt
(ə-dăpt′)
-verb

- After many years of being only a student, I found it hard to **adapt** to the schedule of a full-time job.
- Gina **adapted** well to California. She had no trouble adjusting to living so far from her family and friends.

___ *Adapt* means   a. to return.   b. to become accustomed.   c. to travel.

2 dismay
(dĭs-mā′)
-verb

- Alex was **dismayed** when he realized that he wouldn't have enough money to buy a special birthday present for his girlfriend.
- The doctor knew it would **dismay** Karl to learn that his injured leg would never regain its previous strength.

___ *Dismay* means   a. to discourage.   b. to relieve.   c. to delay.

3 exile
(ĕg′zīl)
-noun

- The political rebel decided to end his five-year **exile** and return to his native land to oppose the government.
- Fernando fled his native country thirty years ago and has lived in **exile** ever since.

___ *Exile* means   a. a long vacation.   b. a bad attitude.   c. a separation from one's homeland.

4 gesture
(jĕs′chər)
-noun

- As a **gesture** of sympathy, the neighborhood association sent flowers to Milly when her husband died.
- The other workers' **gestures** of friendship made Vic feel at home on the first day of his new job.

___ *Gesture* means   a. a sign.   b. a request.   c. a report.

5 recede
(rĭ-sēd′)
-verb

- The heavy blanket of clouds finally began to **recede**, allowing the sun to warm the crowd at the football game.
- Walter had to wait until the flood water **receded** before he could get to his house to see the damage.

___ *Recede* means   a. to grow.   b. to pull back.   c. to return.

6 reciprocate
(rĭ-cĭp′rə-kāt′)
-verb

- I've done many favors for Anne, but she never **reciprocates** by doing a favor in return.
- Alonso treated me to dinner, so I'm going to **reciprocate** by taking him to a movie.

___ *Reciprocate* means   a. to celebrate.   b. to pay back.   c. to disappoint.

7 refute
(rĭ-fyo͞ot′)
-verb

- The lawyer was able to **refute** the defendant's claim that she was home the night of the murder. He had found a witness who saw her in a mall store that night.
- Some science-fiction fans were disappointed when photos of Mars **refuted** the idea that intelligent life exists there.

___ *Refute* means
a. to support.   b. to repeat.   c. to show to be wrong.

8 retain
(rĭ-tān′)
-verb

- Plastic storage containers often **retain** the odors of foods. I have one that still smells like spaghetti sauce after ten washings.
- "I can usually **retain** my sense of humor," Janice said. "But I lose it totally when I'm laid off and break up with my boyfriend in the same week."

___ *Retain* means
a. to hold on to.   b. to adjust to.   c. to lose.

9 revert
(rĭ-vûrt′)
-verb

- After his release from jail, Sam **reverted** to his old habit of stealing and ended up in jail again.
- Helene gave up smoking while she was pregnant, but she **reverted** to a pack a day after her daughter was born.

___ *Revert* means
a. to go back.   b. to refer.   c. to say no.

10 ritual
(rĭch′o͞o-əl)
-noun

- **Rituals**—set practices that are repeated regularly—are important in most religious traditions.
- Each time Mary Ann must fly, she writes a check to a charity, brings it with her on the plane, and mails it at her destination. She believes this **ritual** guarantees a safe flight.

___ *Ritual* means
a. a lesson.   b. a ceremony.   c. a prayer.

Matching Words with Definitions

Following are definitions of the ten words. Clearly write or print each word next to its definition. The sentences above and on the previous page will help you decide on the meaning of each word.

1. _____ To return to a previous habit or condition
2. _____ Something said or done to show intention or attitude
3. _____ To do in return; pay back
4. _____ Separation from one's native country through force or choice
5. _____ A ceremony; any actions done regularly in a set manner
6. _____ To prove wrong or false
7. _____ To adjust to a situation
8. _____ To move back or away from a particular point or limit
9. _____ To keep
10. _____ To discourage; make fearful or uneasy

CAUTION: Do not go any further until you are sure the above answers are correct. Then you can use the definitions to help you in the following practices. Your goal is eventually to know the words well enough so that you don't need to check the definitions at all.

➤ *Sentence Check 1*

Using the answer line provided, complete each item below with the correct word from the box. Use each word once.

a. **adapt**	b. **dismay**	c. **exile**	d. **gesture**	e. **recede**
f. **reciprocate**	g. **refute**	h. **retain**	i. **revert**	j. **ritual**

dismayed   1. Getting a D on the first math test of the semester ___(e)d Sean. He was sure he'd done well.

recede   2. If the shoreline continues to ___, there soon won't be any sandy beach at all.

refute   3. Antonio tried to ___ my argument, but I was able to prove I was right.

gesture   4. In a(n) ___ of cooperation, the manager and the head of the union shook hands.

retain   5. To ___ her strength and energy, Mrs. Green does push-ups, sit-ups, and leg-lifts three times a week.

revert   6. My brother vowed to eat only one Oreo a day, but I'm afraid he'll ___ to his old habit of eating the entire bag of cookies at a sitting.

adapt   7. As the Ice Age ended, some animals were able to ___ to the new climate. Those who could not adjust failed to survive.

Exile   8. The country's new dictator feared having certain political enemies in the country, so he sent them into ___.

reciprocate   9. I always send Karim a birthday card, but he doesn't bother to ___ with a card or phone call on my birthday.

ritual   10. Homer always goes through the same baseball ___ before he bats: he twirls his bat three times, stretches his arms, and says, "Okay, okay, this one will be good."

NOTE: Now check your answers to these questions by turning to page 130. Going over the answers carefully will help you prepare for the next two practices, for which answers are not given.

➤ *Sentence Check 2*

Using the answer lines provided, complete each item below with **two** words from the box. Use each word once.

_____

_____   1–2. "I don't want to ___ you," Jack's lawyer told him. "And I will certainly endeavor° to do my best, but it's going to be difficult to ___ the testimony against you."

_____

_____   3–4. The Reillys have been so kind to me that I want to ___ in some way. I don't have much money, so I hope they'll understand that a small gift is meant as a(n) ___ of great appreciation.

_____   5–6. A reader wrote, "My husband is afraid his hairline will ___, causing
_____   him to ___ to the bald head he was born with." The advice columnist
                                 responded, "Tell him that this obsession° of his shouldn't undermine°
                                 his self-confidence. He's the same great guy with or without hair."

_____   7–8. Any customary ___, such as the Roman Catholic Mass, helps a church
_____   to ___ a sense of tradition.

_____   9–10. The Howards had ___(e)d well to other cultures, but they were still
_____   pleased to retire from the Foreign Service and return to America after
                                  their long ___ in Europe and Asia. Now they love to reminisce° with
                                  their friends about their interesting worldwide adventures.

➤ _Final Check:_ Adjusting to a New Culture

Here is a final opportunity for you to strengthen your knowledge of the ten words. First read the following
selection carefully. Then fill in each blank with a word from the box at the top of the previous page.
(Context clues will help you figure out which word goes in which blank.) Use each word once.

When En-Mei first came to the United States from China, any little problem was enough to

(1)_____ her. As a lonely student, she felt as if she were in forced

(2)_____ from her native country. She didn't like American food and tried to

limit her diet to Chinese dishes. Otherwise, however, she worked hard to (3)_adapt_____

to an unfamiliar country. Finding it difficult to express herself in English, En-Mei at first isolated°

herself from others. But she kept working on her English and eventually became quite fluent° in it.

This helped her to overcome her shyness and learn to (4)_____ other students'

(5)_____s of friendship. When she was with her new friends, homesickness

would (6)_____ into the background.

But En-Mei didn't try to become "all-American"; she wanted to (7)_____

her Chinese identity. She taught her new friends about modern China and tried to

(8)_____ mistaken ideas they had about her country. She even found a group of

friends willing to learn tai chi, an ancient Chinese exercise (9)_____ that benefits

body and spirit. It involves a set series of movements which the group performs together.

Of course, living in America wasn't always easy. Sometimes En-Mei would miss her family so

badly that she would (10)_revert_____ to her former unhappiness. But such times

were increasingly rare. By the end of her first year here, En-Mei even found she had become a

devoted fan of pizza and apple pie.

Scores   Sentence Check 2 _____%   Final Check _____%

Enter your scores above and in the vocabulary performance chart on the inside back cover of the book.

elaborate	indifferent
emerge	indulgent
exotic	liberal
frugal	mediocre
impulsive	notable

Ten Words in Context

In the space provided, write the letter of the meaning closest to that of each **boldfaced** word. Use the context of the sentences to help you figure out each word's meaning.

1 elaborate
(ĭ-lăb′ər-ĭt)
-adjective

- The dinner required **elaborate** preparation. Each course included a complicated favorite dish of one of the guests.
- Irma's quilt was very **elaborate**. She used tiny stitches to sew on the very detailed pattern.

___ *Elaborate* means   a. easy and simple to do.   b. detailed.   c. ordinary.

2 emerge
(ĭ-mûrj′)
-verb

- Anna **emerged** from the dressing room, looking beautiful in a blue prom gown.
- When the chick **emerged** from its egg, it was tired and wet, but a day later it was a fluffy yellow ball of energy.

___ *Emerge* means   a. to come out.   b. to trip.   c. to call out.

3 exotic
(ĭg-zŏt′ĭk)
-adjective

- Orchids are grown in the United States, not just in foreign countries. So Americans really should not consider these flowers **exotic**.
- The kiwi fruit, grown in New Zealand, is one of several **exotic** fruits now commonly sold in supermarkets.

___ *Exotic* means   a. local.   b. foreign.   c. rare.

4 frugal
(frōō′gəl)
-adjective

- You can stretch your dollars by being **frugal**. For example, using store coupons and waiting for expensive items to be on sale can save a lot of money.
- Diane buys designer jeans, but because I need to be more **frugal**, I buy store-brand jeans, which are much cheaper.

___ *Frugal* means   a. hardworking.   b. lucky.   c. thrifty.

5 impulsive
(ĭm-pŭl′sĭv)
-adjective

- Ved is too **impulsive** to make plans. He always prefers to act on the spur of the moment.
- Kids are usually more **impulsive** than adults. Children will follow such sudden urges as the desire to climb a tree even if they are wearing their best clothes.

___ *Impulsive* means   a. fearful.   b. careful.   c. acting without planning.

6 indifferent
(ĭn-dĭf′ər-ənt)
-adjective

- Does our society have no interest in homeless children? Are we **indifferent** to the many families who can no longer afford to pay rent?
- Because her husband was **indifferent** to how the apartment would be decorated, Kathy felt free to do the job any way she wanted.

___ *Indifferent to* means   a. interested in.   b. unconcerned with.   c. insulted by.

7 indulgent
(ĭn-dŭl′jənt)
-adjective

- Monica's grandparents are too **indulgent** with her. They don't scold her even when she splatters the walls with baby food.
- I'm surprised at Robin's self-**indulgent** attitude. It never occurs to her not to give in to every little desire she has.

___ *Indulgent* means   a. strict.   b. giving.   c. not caring.

8 liberal
(lĭb′ər-əl)
-adjective

- Being a chocolate lover, Amos puts **liberal** amounts of chocolate chips in his Toll House cookies.
- Norma left the waiter a **liberal** tip because he had been especially friendly and helpful.

___ *Liberal* means   a. average.   b. frequent.   c. generous.

9 mediocre
(mē-dē-ō′kər)
-adjective

- The mystery movie was neither terrible nor great; it was **mediocre**.
- Although Hank can be quite funny, his jokes are only **mediocre** compared with those of the best comedians.

___ *Mediocre* means   a. ordinary.   b. awful.   c. short.

10 notable
(nō′tə-bəl)
-adjective

- Winning the Nobel Prize can make a little-known scientist into a **notable** world figure.
- Abraham Lincoln's "Gettysburg Address" is surely his most **notable** speech, especially among the many Americans who memorized it in school.

___ *Notable* means   a. ineffective.   b. well-known.   c. generous.

Matching Words with Definitions

Following are definitions of the ten words. Clearly write or print each word next to its definition. The sentences above and on the previous page will help you decide on the meaning of each word.

1. _____   To rise up or come forth

2. _____   Famous; widely known

3. _____   Having no real interest; unconcerned

4. _____   Large in amount or quantity; generous

5. _____   Done with great attention to details; complicated

6. _____   Average; ordinary; neither very bad nor very good

7. _____   Tending to act on sudden urges; not in the habit of planning ahead

8. _____   Foreign; from a different part of the world; strange or different in an appealing way

9. _____   Thrifty; avoiding unnecessary expenses

10. _____   Giving in to someone's desires, often too much so

CAUTION: Do not go any further until you are sure the above answers are correct. Then you can use the definitions to help you in the following practices. Your goal is eventually to know the words well enough so that you don't need to check the definitions at all.

➤ *Sentence Check 1*

Using the answer line provided, complete each item below with the correct word from the box. Use each word once.

a. **elaborate**	b. **emerge**	c. **exotic**	d. **frugal**	e. **impulsive**
f. **indifferent**	g. **indulgent**	h. **liberal**	i. **mediocre**	j. **notable**

_____ 1. Although my father didn't do badly in school, he wasn't a great student. So he's proof it's possible to have a successful career despite ___ grades.

_____ 2. Overly ___ parents, who let young children do whatever they please, will end up with problem teenagers.

_____ 3. The puppy ___(e)d from her bath much cleaner than when she entered it, but we doubted that she'd stay clean for long.

_____ 4. Greg is such a skilled public speaker that we all expect him to become a ___ politician one day.

_____ 5. The boss gave such ___ bonuses that Gail was able to buy a new sofa with the money.

_____ 6. Ella embroidered a(n) ___ design on the back of her sweatshirt. She used four colors in a complicated pattern of swirls and flowers.

_____ 7. People walked past the bleeding, moaning man without even pausing; they were ___ to his need for help.

_____ 8. "Gowns are so expensive," Mimi said, "that I've decided to be ___ and rent a wedding dress instead of buying one."

_____ 9. Bruce, as ___ as ever, suddenly changed his mind about going to a restaurant and announced, "Let's have a picnic."

_____ 10. A Native American rain dance may seem ___ to many people in the United States, but it is actually more native to this country than square-dancing.

NOTE: Now check your answers to these questions by turning to page 130. Going over the answers carefully will help you prepare for the next two practices, for which answers are not given.

➤ *Sentence Check 2*

Using the answer lines provided, complete each item below with **two** words from the box. Use each word once.

_____
_____ 1–2. The actress, ___ for her great performance, deserved her Academy Award. Compared with her, all of the others appeared ___. Overjoyed, she said, "Thank you, thank you, thank you. This is my first Oscar, and I am too thrilled to think of anything else to say."

_____ 3–4. Every time Sylvia shops, she manages to ___ from the store without a single unnecessary purchase. I wish I could be such a(n) ___ shopper.

_____ 5–6. The ___ meal, full of strange but delicious foods, involved ___
_____   preparation that took up most of the afternoon.

_____ 7–8. When it comes to the suffering of others, Americans are idealistic°.
_____   When a disaster strikes, they find it difficult to be ___ to the victims, so
                                         they send ___ donations to the Red Cross.

_____ 9–10. Rafael is so ___ that he often decides he wants to go out for dinner or to
_____   a movie at the last minute. Overly ___, his wife agrees every time. She
                                          even defers° to his wish to eat out after she has already cooked dinner.

➤ *Final Check:* A Dream About Wealth

Here is a final opportunity for you to strengthen your knowledge of the ten words. First read the following selection carefully. Then fill in each blank with a word from the box at the top of the previous page. (Context clues will help you figure out which word goes in which blank.) Use each word once.

In my student days, when I was very poor, I sometimes daydreamed about being very rich. I imagined being such a(n) (1)_____ member of society that my name would turn up in the newspaper columns every time I attended a party. I pictured myself traveling to (2)_____ places in faraway lands and being a patron° of the finest restaurants. I would forget no detail when planning (3)_____ parties for five hundred of my closest friends. There would be nothing (4)_____ in my life, not even an ordinary, average toaster. No, I would have the finest toasters, the biggest houses, the most glamorous wardrobe—the best. And I would own a unique° art collection—no prints for me, only one-of-a-kind masterpieces by famous artists. Of course, I would be quite (5)_____: whenever I had the urge, I would buy diamond jewelry or jump into my Olympic-size pool. But I promised myself that I wouldn't be totally self-(6)_____. I'd also give (7)_____ amounts of money to help the poor and underprivileged. I would not be (8)_____ to their needs. And being modest as well as generous, I'd always be an anonymous° donor°.

After graduating, I began saving money, and I stopped daydreaming about being rich. Having some earnings to spend, I had finally (9)_____(e)d from a life of endless budgeting, a life in which I was forced to be extremely (10)_____. Of course, I am still thrifty because I don't want to waste my hard-earned money. But now that I have enough money to be comfortable, I no longer daydream about being super-rich.

Scores	Sentence Check 2 _____%	Final Check _____%

Enter your scores above and in the vocabulary performance chart on the inside back cover of the book.

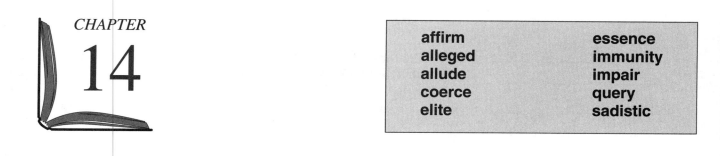

CHAPTER 14

affirm	essence
alleged	immunity
allude	impair
coerce	query
elite	sadistic

Ten Words in Context

In the space provided, write the letter of the meaning closest to that of each **boldfaced** word. Use the context of the sentences to help you figure out each word's meaning.

1 **affirm**
(ə-fûrm′)
-verb

- The witness **affirmed** in court that he had seen the defendant commit the robbery.
- Lana did **affirm** during the wedding ceremony that she would love and honor Joseph, but she did not state that she would obey him.

___ *Affirm* means
    a. to fear.   b. to state.   c. to write.

2 **alleged**
(ə-lĕjd′)
-adjective

- The **alleged** killer was never proven guilty in court, but many people believe he committed the murder.
- Nan, who believed Luther was innocent of starting the fire, reminded her friends that his guilt was only **alleged**.

___ *Alleged* means
    a. assumed.   b. admired.   c. harmless.

3 **allude**
(ə-lood′)
-verb

- Although the mayor won't name her opponent, she plans to **allude** to him by mentioning the scandal he's involved in.
- Regina **alluded** to Sal's weight gain by calling him "Santa."

___ *Allude to* means
    a. to clearly mention.   b. to hint at.   c. to keep.

4 **coerce**
(kō-ûrs′)
-verb

- To **coerce** the general into giving up, the rebels kidnapped his daughter.
- Our gym teacher used to **coerce** us into doing fifty sit-ups by refusing to let anyone leave before we all had finished.

___ *Coerce* means
    a. to talk.   b. to join.   c. to force.

5 **elite**
(ĭ-lēt′)
-adjective

- The 57th was the **elite** military unit. Its members were the toughest and the smartest and had trained the longest.
- The **elite** neighborhood in town is surrounded by a high fence and has a guard at its gates.

___ *Elite* means
    a. worst.   b. best.   c. least important.

6 **essence**
(ĕs′əns)
-noun

- Trust is the **essence** of a good relationship; without it, the relationship won't last.
- Boiled down to its **essence**, the lecture can be stated in one short sentence: Much important work gets done in America by volunteers.

___ *Essence* means
    a. the main part.   b. the opposite.   c. the sad part.

7 **immunity**
(ĭ-myo͞o′nĭ-tē)
-noun

- Foreign ambassadors often park in no-parking zones because they ~~ **immunity** from parking fines.
- When the actor punched a police officer, even his wealth and fame didn't get him **immunity** from jail.

___ *Immunity* means   a. recognition.   b. freedom.   c. an income.

8 **impair**
(ĭm-pâr′)
-verb

- Listening to loud music **impairs** hearing by damaging the inner ear.
- The rifle shot didn't kill the deer, but it **impaired** her running ability, leaving her with a limp.

___ *Impair* means   a. to involve.   b. to repair.   c. to harm.

9 **query**
(kwēr′ē)
-verb

- If no printed schedule is available, please **query** the person at the information booth to learn the time of your train's arrival or departure.
- Reporters repeatedly **queried** the president about taxes, but his only reply was "No comment."

___ *Query* means   a. to ask.   b. to quote.   c. to answer.

10 **sadistic**
(sə-dĭs′tĭk)
-adjective

- Cats seem to be naturally **sadistic**. Instead of killing their victims quickly, they like to make the process slow and drawn-out.
- Our **sadistic** science teacher had a strange way of teaching about electrical currents. First, he had us hold hands in a circle. Then he put one student's hand on a wire with a slight electrical charge.

___ *Sadistic* means   a. sad.   b. cruel.   c. rude.

Matching Words with Definitions

Following are definitions of the ten words. Clearly write or print each word next to its definition. The sentences above and on the previous page will help you decide on the meaning of each word.

1. _____   To damage; weaken

2. _____   To refer indirectly

3. _____   Taking pleasure from being cruel

4. _____   A fundamental characteristic or the most important quality of something; the heart of a matter

5. _____   Freedom from something unpleasant or something required of others

6. _____   To indicate to be true; state with certainty

7. _____   Being or intended for the best or most privileged; superior

8. _____   To force; compel°

9. _____   Supposed to be true or real, but not proved; assumed

10. _____   To question; ask

CAUTION: Do not go any further until you are sure the above answers are correct. Then you can use the definitions to help you in the following practices. Your goal is eventually to know the words well enough so that you don't need to check the definitions at all.

➣ *Sentence Check 1*

Using the answer line provided, complete each item below with the correct word from the box. Use each word once.

a. **affirm**	b. **alleged**	c. **allude**	d. **coerce**	e. **elite**
f. **essence**	g. **immunity**	h. **impair**	i. **query**	j. **sadistic**

_____ 1. The Puritan colonists ___(e)d Native Americans into slavery by capturing and selling them to buyers in the West Indies.

_____ 2. The ___ war criminal had laughed while he tortured his victims.

_____ 3. Drugs and alcohol ___ a person's ability to drive.

_____ 4. The ___ of a paragraph is stated in its topic sentence.

_____ 5. As a child, I didn't enjoy total ___ from punishment, but my parents rarely spanked me.

_____ 6. During the spelling bee, the judge would ___ that a spelling was correct by nodding silently.

_____ 7. The ___ car thief could not possibly be guilty. Not only was he out of town on the day of the theft, but he cannot drive.

_____ 8. A(n) ___ group of doctors, including the country's top brain surgeons, met to discuss a new operation.

_____ 9. When two people are arrested for the same crime, the police ___ them separately to see if they give the same answers.

_____ 10. My brother and I used secret names to ___ to certain relatives. For example, if we wished to speak about Aunt Dotty, we instead spoke about "an old Chevy."

NOTE: Now check your answers to these questions by turning to page 130. Going over the answers carefully will help you prepare for the next two practices, for which answers are not given.

➣ *Sentence Check 2*

Using the answer lines provided, complete each item below with **two** words from the box. Use each word once.

_____
_____ 1–2. The senator would neither deny nor ___ that the ___, expensive country club he belonged to allowed no minority members. Nevertheless, to avoid any appearance of a problem, he decided it would be appropriate° to resign from the club.

_____
_____ 3–4. I need to ___ my teacher more closely about her views on protecting the environment. Although I've grasped the ___ of her position, I don't understand all the details yet.

_____ 5–6. When my roommate wants to ___ me into doing her some favor, all she
_____ has to do is ___ to certain dark secrets of mine. The hint that she might
tell them leaves me no option° but to help her out.

_____ 7–8. One terrible beating by her ___ husband was enough to ___ the
_____ woman's sight for life. That's when she decided to get help, before one
of his attacks became lethal°.

_____ 9–10. Nobody is sure if the ___ bribery really took place. The person who
_____ would have been the chief suspect was given ___ from arrest by a
powerful political figure.

➤ *Final Check:* Children and Drugs

Here is a final opportunity for you to strengthen your knowledge of the ten words. First read the following
selection carefully. Then fill in each blank with a word from the box at the top of the previous page.
(Context clues will help you figure out which word goes in which blank.) Use each word once.

When I hear people talk about "harmless, recreational" drug use, it makes me sick. It isn't
only because I'm concerned about what the drug users are doing to their own minds and bodies.
It's because I've seen the business that these people are supporting with their "recreational" drug
use. It's a business run by the scum of the earth—people so evil and (1)_____
that they will gladly use children as human shields between themselves and the law.

On a daily basis in our nation's cities, police pick up preteens who are used as drug dealers'
lookouts and delivery boys. When the police (2)_____ them, the children often
say that the dealers (3)_____ them into doing these jobs. Because they are so
afraid of the dealers, they usually don't say very much more. They may (4)_____
to "bad things" happening to children who cooperate with police. Police know that those "bad
things" often include being beaten, tortured, and even killed.

Sadly, poor kids don't always need to be forced. They are naturally attracted to the money that is
offered, and they speak of the dealers with awe°. In neighborhoods where honest jobs are scarce, the
dealers, with their fancy cars and rolls of money, seem to these children to be members of a(n)
(5)_____ club. According to the mother of one (6)_____ drug
delivery boy (the police could never prove he really was a drug runner), the dealers serve as "role
models" to her son and his friends.

The dealers, of course, take full advantage of these children and their poverty. The kids are
useful to the dealers because their age gives them (7)_____ from serious
criminal charges. The police (8)_____ that arresting the children doesn't
(9)_____ the dealers' business much. The loss of a child or two is not important
to the dealers, because it doesn't inhibit° other poor, eager kids who are ready to take the lost child's
place. To the children, at least at first, serving as lookouts and drug runners is almost a game. By the
time they find out what kind of evil, malicious° people they are working for, it is too late to get out.

As the "recreational" drug users sit safely in their comfortable homes, enjoying their
"harmless" highs, I hope they think of these children. The children's ruined lives clearly show that
the (10)_____ of the drug trade is the abuse of people.

| *Scores* | Sentence Check 2 _____% | Final Check _____% |

Enter your scores above and in the vocabulary performance chart on the inside back cover of the book.

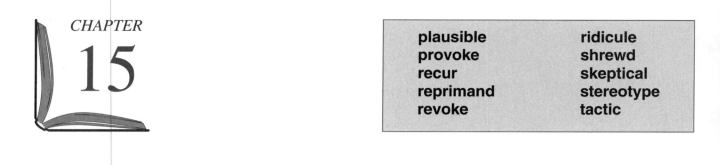

plausible	ridicule
provoke	shrewd
recur	skeptical
reprimand	stereotype
revoke	tactic

Ten Words in Context

In the space provided, write the letter of the meaning closest to that of each **boldfaced** word. Use the context of the sentences to help you figure out each word's meaning.

1 **plausible**
(plô'zə-bəl)
-adjective

- Was Buck's excuse for being late **plausible**? Or did he tell you some unbelievable story?
- "Some TV shows are just not **plausible**," said the producer. "Who ever heard of a flying nun or a teenage doctor?"

___ *Plausible* means
   a. nice.
   b. believable.
   c. long enough.

2 **provoke**
(prə-vōk')
-verb

- "Mr. Jackson **provoked** me by saying nasty things about my mother, so I hit him," Terry told the judge.
- My father is slow to anger, but this morning my sister's wisecracks began to **provoke** him.

___ *Provoke* means
   a. to delay.
   b. to confuse.
   c. to anger.

3 **recur**
(rĭ-kûr')
-verb

- Five-year-old Arnie's nightmare of ghosts chasing him tends to **recur** at least once a week.
- "If your headaches keep **recurring**," the doctor told Mrs. Lopez, "I'm going to recommend a lab test. We need to find out why you are having so much pain."

___ *Recur* means
   a. to disappear.
   b. to improve.
   c. to happen again.

4 **reprimand**
(rĕp'rə-mănd')
-noun

- If a boss wants to criticize a worker, the union requires that the **reprimand** be written.
- As a child, when I misbehaved, my father gave me verbal **reprimands**, but my mother would not hesitate to give me a slap on the rear end.

___ *Reprimand* means
   a. praise.
   b. a scolding.
   c. an answer.

5 **revoke**
(rĭ-vōk')
-verb

- Mrs. Byers said she would **revoke** Ken's privileges at the computer lab if he ever again squirted glue between the computer keys.
- To avoid having his driver's license **revoked**, Art paid the $467 he owed for all of his speeding tickets.

___ *Revoke* means
   a. to cancel.
   b. to make longer.
   c. to recognize.

6 **ridicule**
(rĭd'ĭ-kyool')
-verb

- Ignorant people often **ridicule** my brother because he is so overweight. Even if they had perfect bodies—which they do not—they have no right to tease him.
- Eugene knew his friends would **ridicule** him for wearing a shirt and shorts with two different plaids, but he had no other clean clothes to wear.

___ *Ridicule* means
   a. to praise.
   b. to notice.
   c. to make fun of.

7 shrewd
(shrōōd)
-adjective

- Eddie is a fine musician, but he's no good with money. So he hired a friend with a **shrewd** business sense to handle his financial affairs.
- Sherry is a **shrewd** chess player. She always surprises her opponents with clever winning moves.

___ *Shrewd* means   a. lucky.   b. loud.   c. smart.

8 skeptical
(skĕp′tĭ-kəl)
-adjective

- Jessica's family is so rich that she is **skeptical** about any man who asks her out. She wonders if he's interested in her or in her money.
- I am **skeptical** about the articles on movie stars and space aliens in supermarket newspapers. My brother, however, believes every word he reads in those papers.

___ *Skeptical* means   a. economical.   b. doubtful.   c. believing.

9 stereotype
(stĕr′ē-ə-tīp′)
-noun

- Bev still accepts the **stereotype** of all athletes as dumb even though the school's star quarterback is her math tutor.
- Because not all members of a group are alike, **stereotypes** lead to inaccurate judgments of people.

___ *Stereotype* means   a. an oversimplified image.   b. a desired image.   c. a true image.

10 tactic
(tăk′tĭc)
-noun

- The teacher finally caught on to Greg's sneaky **tactic** for getting his homework done—having his sister do it.
- The best **tactic** for keeping young children from fighting is to separate them.

___ *Tactic* means   a. a method.   b. a result.   c. a reason.

Matching Words with Definitions

Following are definitions of the ten words. Clearly write or print each word next to its definition. The sentences above and on the previous page will help you decide on the meaning of each word.

1. _____ Doubting; questioning

2. _____ Clever; tricky

3. _____ Believable; appearing truthful or reasonable

4. _____ To stir up anger or resentment

5. _____ To take away or cancel

6. _____ A means to reach a goal; method

7. _____ A formal criticism; a harsh scolding

8. _____ To make fun of; mock

9. _____ To occur again; happen repeatedly

10. _____ A commonly accepted image that is oversimplified, with no individuality taken into account

CAUTION: Do not go any further until you are sure the above answers are correct. Then you can use the definitions to help you in the following practices. Your goal is eventually to know the words well enough so that you don't need to check the definitions at all.

➤ *Sentence Check 1*

Using the answer line provided, complete each item below with the correct word from the box. Use each word once.

a. plausible	b. provoke	c. recur	d. reprimand	e. revoke
f. ridicule	g. shrewd	h. skeptical	i. stereotype	j. tactic

_____ 1. At first the other students ___(e)d Sofi for speaking with an accent, but they stopped teasing her once they got to know her better.

_____ 2. Aesop's Fables are charming stories based on ___s of animals. In the fables, foxes are always sly, lions are always fierce, and owls are always wise.

_____ 3. It takes great skill to make a science fiction film seem ___ to the audience.

_____ 4. It was ___ of Connie to move to California last year. Now she can pay in-state fees when she takes courses at San Bernardino Valley College.

_____ 5. Jordan has headaches that ___ as often as once a day.

_____ 6. Some divorced parents who want to see more of their children use an illegal ___: kidnapping.

_____ 7. The roofer's estimate was so low that we became ___ about the quality of his work.

_____ 8. The principal wrote our gym teacher a note of ___ for not having his class leave the gym right after the fire alarm rang.

_____ 9. Angelo usually doesn't let his older sister's teasing ___ him, but he gets angry whenever she calls him "baby."

_____ 10. Eleanor's parents said she could not attend the prom because of her bad grades, but later they felt sorry for her and ___(e)d the punishment.

NOTE: Now check your answers to these questions by turning to page 130. Going over the answers carefully will help you prepare for the next two practices, for which answers are not given.

➤ *Sentence Check 2*

Using the answer lines provided, complete each item below with **two** words from the box. Use each word once.

_____
_____ 1–2. When it comes to preventing cheating, our science teacher is ___. His ___s include checking our hands before a test and having us sit in alternate seats during a test. And he puts students he's suspicious of in prominent° seats near the front of the room.

_____
_____ 3–4. Some ___s may get their start when certain behavior patterns ___ among members of a particular group.

_____ 5–6. "Of course I'm ___ about your excuse," Mel's boss said. "You have to
_____   give me a more ___ reason for not calculating the sales figures than
                                  that you couldn't find a pen or pencil."

_____ 7–8. "It is illegal to park your hot-dog cart in a McDonald's driveway," said
_____   the judge to the owner of the cart. "This time you're getting only a ___.
                                  Next time your license may be ___(e)d."

_____ 9–10. When some boys teased and ___(e)d a learning-disabled student for
_____   being "dumb," the principal was greatly ___(e)d. So she kept the boys
                                  after school and compelled° them to write "I am not as smart as I
                                  think" five hundred times.

➤ _Final Check:_ Party House

Here is a final opportunity for you to strengthen your knowledge of the ten words. First read the following
selection carefully. Then fill in each blank with a word from the box at the top of the previous page.
(Context clues will help you figure out which word goes in which blank.) Use each word once.

The loud parties at the Phi Gamma fraternity house had (1)_____(e)d its

neighbors all year. The neighbors complained to the college, but the Phi Gammas were

(2)_____ enough to come up with a (3)_____ explanation

each time. Each explanation, of course, was an elaborate° lie. For example, they once claimed that

one of their members tended to have nightmares which would (4)_____

throughout finals week, making him cry out loudly throughout the night. This, they said, woke up

all of the other members, who had gone to bed early that evening. Again and again, the Phi

Gammas were let off by the lenient° college dean with only a (5)_____. But

members of the other fraternities were (6)_____ about Phi Gamma's excuses.

They also disliked the way the group contributed to a negative (7)_____ of

fraternities. So they decided on a (8)_____ to get back at Phi Gamma. They

secretly tape-recorded one of the Phi Gamma meetings. During that meeting, the Phi Gamma

members (9)_____(e)d the dean by mocking the way he always believed their

excuses. And, still indifferent° to the comfort of their neighbors, they also made plans for more

loud parties. When the dean heard the recording, he (10)_____(e)d Phi

Gamma's campus license.

Scores Sentence Check 2 _____%	Final Check _____%

Enter your scores above and in the vocabulary performance chart on the inside back cover of the book.

UNIT THREE: Review

The box at the right lists twenty-five words from Unit Three. Using the clues at the bottom of the page, fill in these words to complete the puzzle that follows.

adapt
allude
coerce
elaborate
emerge
equate
essence
exile
immunity
impulsive
indignant
liberal
malicious
mediocre
passive
patron
plausible
provoke
recede
recur
refute
revert
sadistic
stereotype
tactic

ACROSS

1. Separation from one's native country
5. Average; ordinary; neither very bad nor very good
7. Believable; appearing truthful or reasonable
8. Being acted upon without acting in return
11. Showing great ill will; mean; deliberately harmful
12. A commonly accepted image that is oversimplified, with no individuality taken into account
16. To refer indirectly
19. To return to a previous habit or condition
20. To stir up anger or resentment
22. To adjust to a situation
23. To force; compel
24. To rise up or come forth
25. To prove wrong or false

DOWN

2. Angry because of some insult or injustice
3. Large in amount or quantity; generous
4. Tending to act on sudden urges; not in the habit of planning ahead
6. Taking pleasure from being cruel
9. Freedom from something unpleasant or something required of others
10. Done with great attention to details; complicated
13. To consider to be equal, the same, or similar
14. A means to reach a goal; method
15. A customer, especially a steady one
17. A fundamental characteristic; the most important quality of something; the heart of a matter
18. To move back or away from a particular point or limit
21. To occur again; happen repeatedly

UNIT THREE: Test 1

PART A
Choose the word that best completes each item and write it in the space provided.

_____ 1. After my brother gave me the measles, I ___ by giving him the mumps.

    a. adapted   b. coerced   c. provoked   d. reciprocated

_____ 2. It may not seem ___, but it's true—some people need only fifteen minutes of sleep a day.

    a. frugal   b. plausible   c. elaborate   d. liberal

_____ 3. A bee will usually not sting unless you first ___ it—for example, by swatting at it.

    a. adapt   b. retain   c. provoke   d. allude

_____ 4. Many ___ shoppers buy soy-based foods because they are inexpensive sources of protein.

    a. indifferent   b. plausible   c. frugal   d. sadistic

_____ 5. The singer's voice is only ___, but he's very popular because his personality is so appealing.

    a. notable   b. mediocre   c. exotic   d. elite

_____ 6. Although the police report mentioned a(n) ___ "break-in," the gold theft may actually have been an "inside" job.

    a. tedious   b. indulgent   c. alleged   d. indifferent

_____ 7. We considered several ___ for dinner: cooking, going out, or having a pizza delivered.

    a. patrons   b. options   c. rituals   d. stereotypes

_____ 8. My teacher meant to ___, "Why did you miss the history lecture?" Instead he asked, "Why did you hiss the mystery lecture?"

    a. adapt   b. dismay   c. query   d. allude

_____ 9. When the usually peppy dog became ___ and wouldn't play, Marta knew he must be ill.

    a. skeptical   b. passive   c. indignant   d. shrewd

_____ 10. Experts have ___ the idea that giant redwood trees are the oldest living things on Earth. Certain pine trees that are about 4,600 years of age are now known to be older.

    a. refuted   b. coerced   c. emerged   d. provoked

(Continues on next page)

PART B

On the answer line, write the letter of the choice that best completes each item.

_____ 11. I **equate** our school's great basketball team
  a. with some professional teams.   b. in the newspaper each morning.
  c. by attending its games.   d. because I work on game nights.

_____ 12. To **defer** to my parents' wishes that I dress up for Thanksgiving dinner, I
  a. went barefoot.   b. wore a turkey costume.
  c. wore a tie.   d. skipped the dinner.

_____ 13. A **malicious** reply to the question "Will you go out with me on Friday?" is
  a. "No, thank you; I have other plans."   b. "Why would I do that? You're disgusting."
  c. "I'd really like to go out with you."   d. "I'm not sure if I'm free that night."

_____ 14. Diners **emerge** from a restaurant
  a. to look for something to eat.   b. after they have finished their meals.
  c. only if they have liked the food.   d. according to its price, selection, and quality.

_____ 15. One **gesture** of friendship is
  a. offering to treat your friend to a meal.   b. two people having many things in common.
  c. screening incoming phone calls.   d. not having time to spend with friends.

_____ 16. **Sadistic** people are often the main characters in
  a. picture books.   b. horror movies.
  c. TV sitcoms.   d. romantic comedies.

_____ 17. When he was told that the pay for his summer job would be **liberal**, Sammy said,
  a. "I can't afford to work for so little. I'll have to find another job."
  b. "It's not much, but I guess it will be OK."
  c. "Why are you paying me only once a month?"
  d. "Wonderful! I didn't expect to earn that much."

_____ 18. Naturally, the child received a **reprimand** when she
  a. purposely smashed her grandmother's favorite vase.
  b. rescued her little brother from the swimming pool.
  c. asked if she could have a puppy for her birthday.
  d. hugged her father when he lost his job, telling him, "Your boss is a naughty man."

_____ 19. The new beauty salon, Scissors Palace, is so **elite** that
  a. neighborhood kids go there for haircuts.
  b. people can get their hair done there without an appointment.
  c. most of its clients are celebrities.
  d. nobody goes there more than once—its stylists are terrible.

_____ 20. Greta **alluded** to the size of the rich woman's five-carat diamond ring by
  a. saying, "Is it hailing tonight? Someone seems to have a big chunk of ice stuck to her hand."
  b. exclaiming in a loud voice, "Good grief, look at the size of that diamond!"
  c. asking the woman if she had had the ring for a long time.
  d. ignoring the woman and her ring completely.

Score   (Number correct) _____ x 5 = _____ %

Enter your score above and in the vocabulary performance chart on the inside back cover of the book.

UNIT THREE: Test 2

PART A
Complete each item with a word from the box. Use each word once.

a. **adapt**	b. **coerce**	c. **elaborate**	d. **essence**	e. **exile**
f. **impose**	g. **indignant**	h. **indulgent**	i. **recur**	j. **retain**
k. **revert**	l. **stereotype**	m. **tactic**		

_____ 1. After recently lending Trisha money to help her pay her rent, I was ___ when I learned she had been using the money to buy herself expensive jewelry.

_____ 2. The ___ dollhouse included many realistic details, such as tiny lamps, clocks, and flowers in vases.

_____ 3. The ___ of a thunderstorm is energy—energy sometimes equal to that of a dozen atomic bombs.

_____ 4. To make sure the hamstring injury does not ___, always stretch your leg muscles before working out.

_____ 5. My sister ___s on her husband's good nature by having him run errands for her all the time.

_____ 6. The ___ of the cowboy is that of a rough and romantic fighter, but most cowboys actually spent their days doing routine chores.

_____ 7. A well-known Chinese author had to leave his homeland to avoid being imprisoned. He was forced into ___ for attacking the Chinese government in his writings.

_____ 8. On New Year's Eve I decided to stop eating chocolate, but by January 4th I ___(e)d to my old ways—stocking up on on Mars bars and M&M's.

_____ 9. Deaf people have ___(e)d to today's technology in clever ways. For example, they use vibrating wireless pagers as their cell phones.

_____ 10. Many students have used the ___ of blaming the computer for their missed deadlines. They say, for example, "It erased my whole paper."

_____ 11. In ancient Rome, some of the wealthiest and most self-___ people powdered their hair every day with pure gold dust.

_____ 12. Built of white marble and decorated with gems, the famous Taj Mahal of India has ___(e)d its beauty for more than three hundred years.

_____ 13. Because a thief might ___ you into handing over a wallet, carry an extra one with little money, an old ID card, and out-of-date credit cards.

(Continues on next page)

PART B
Write **C** if the italicized word is used **correctly**. Write **I** if the word is used **incorrectly**.

_____ 14. Judging by the smile of relief on his face, the x-ray *dismayed* Dr. Ali.

_____ 15. Iris is so *impulsive* that she won't even take a step outside without first listening to a weather report.

_____ 16. If you're entering a movie theater with a crowd, it's *shrewd* to go left. Since most people head right, you'll get a better choice of seats that way.

_____ 17. The construction company had its license *revoked* when its materials were found to be dangerously weak.

_____ 18. My brother used to *ridicule* me for talking on the phone so much. He would holler, "Get a doctor! A phone is growing out of Stacy's head."

_____ 19. Gina and Steve are *patrons* of the local Japanese restaurant. They eat there every Friday night.

_____ 20. The Liberty Bell, so *exotic* to all Americans, was once offered for sale as scrap metal.

_____ 21. A tornado's winds can *recede* to speeds as high as two hundred miles an hour.

_____ 22. I was *skeptical* when the salesman said I could get a month's worth of frozen food for under fifty dollars a person.

_____ 23. Anyone who needs a wheelchair is bound to be *indifferent* to a new one that is able to follow spoken instructions.

_____ 24. Bob *endeavored* to save the diseased tree, saying, "Let's just chop it down for firewood."

_____ 25. Although most *notable* as a scientist, Albert Einstein was also well known as a spokesman for world peace.

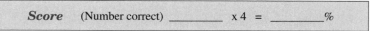

| *Score*   (Number correct) _____   x 4 = _____% |

Enter your score above and in the vocabulary performance chart on the inside back cover of the book.

UNIT THREE: Test 3

PART A: Synonyms
In the space provided, write the letter of the choice that is most nearly the **same** in meaning as the **boldfaced** word.

_____ 1. **ritual**   **a)** sign   **b)** adjustment   **c)** ceremony   **d)** wealth

_____ 2. **patron**   **a)** customer   **b)** employer   **c)** voter   **d)** owner

_____ 3. **coerce**   **a)** force   **b)** join   **c)** deny   **d)** support

_____ 4. **impose on**   **a)** uninterested in   **b)** keep   **c)** take advantage of   **d)** take away from

_____ 5. **endeavor**   **a)** repay   **b)** try   **c)** leave   **d)** repeat

_____ 6. **option**   **a)** main quality   **b)** question   **c)** method   **d)** choice

_____ 7. **adapt**   **a)** disprove   **b)** consider equal   **c)** adjust   **d)** inform

_____ 8. **reprimand**   **a)** criticism   **b)** repetition   **c)** separation   **d)** reminder

_____ 9. **reciprocate**   **a)** repeat   **b)** approve   **c)** repay   **d)** keep

_____ 10. **equate**   **a)** multiply   **b)** consider equal   **c)** appear   **d)** force

_____ 11. **gesture**   **a)** question   **b)** method   **c)** doubt   **d)** action showing one's attitude

_____ 12. **recur**   **a)** happen again   **b)** pay back   **c)** discourage   **d)** respect

_____ 13. **allude**   **a)** mislead   **b)** refer indirectly   **c)** make ineffective   **d)** attract

_____ 14. **exile**   **a)** equality   **b)** harm   **c)** separation from home   **d)** travel

_____ 15. **refute**   **a)** support   **b)** disprove   **c)** admit   **d)** refuse

_____ 16. **tactic**   **a)** effort   **b)** criticism   **c)** central quality   **d)** method

_____ 17. **indignant**   **a)** angry   **b)** cruel   **c)** doubtful   **d)** generous

_____ 18. **essence**   **a)** protection   **b)** question   **c)** search   **d)** heart of a matter

_____ 19. **shrewd**   **a)** clear   **b)** simple   **c)** clever   **d)** stupid

_____ 20. **stereotype**   **a)** alternative   **b)** oversimplified image   **c)** ceremony   **d)** effort

_____ 21. **defer**   **a)** yield   **b)** oppose   **c)** move up   **d)** change

_____ 22. **revert**   **a)** anger   **b)** go back   **c)** reply   **d)** rise

_____ 23. **ridicule**   **a)** remove   **b)** ruin   **c)** brag about   **d)** make fun of

_____ 24. **alleged**   **a)** clear   **b)** proven   **c)** supposed   **d)** inactive

_____ 25. **immunity**   **a)** anger   **b)** fear   **c)** requirement   **d)** freedom

(Continues on next page)

PART B: Antonyms

In the space provided, write the letter of the choice that is most nearly the **opposite** in meaning to the **boldfaced** word.

_____ 26. **skeptical**   **a)** respectful   **b)** equal   **c)** dull   **d)** convinced

_____ 27. **emerge**   **a)** disappear   **b)** improve   **c)** appear   **d)** harm

_____ 28. **liberal**   **a)** simple   **b)** clever   **c)** cheap   **d)** pleased

_____ 29. **elaborate**   **a)** foreign   **b)** uninterested   **c)** kind   **d)** simple

_____ 30. **frugal**   **a)** wasteful   **b)** special   **c)** ordinary   **d)** angry

_____ 31. **notable**   **a)** complicated   **b)** unknown   **c)** excellent   **d)** active

_____ 32. **retain**   **a)** admit   **b)** give away   **c)** contain   **d)** take advantage of

_____ 33. **query**   **a)** appear   **b)** admire   **c)** refer   **d)** answer

_____ 34. **affirm**   **a)** happen once   **b)** deny   **c)** separate   **d)** support

_____ 35. **passive**   **a)** known   **b)** generous   **c)** ordinary   **d)** active

_____ 36. **impair**   **a)** double   **b)** reverse   **c)** improve   **d)** answer

_____ 37. **elite**   **a)** worst   **b)** foreign   **c)** natural   **d)** playful

_____ 38. **inevitable**   **a)** unknown   **b)** believable   **c)** avoidable   **d)** simple

_____ 39. **dismay**   **a)** encourage   **b)** disprove   **c)** disappoint   **d)** find

_____ 40. **mediocre**   **a)** active   **b)** pleased   **c)** excellent   **d)** unbelievable

_____ 41. **indifferent**   **a)** odd   **b)** interested   **c)** ordinary   **d)** disappointed

_____ 42. **sadistic**   **a)** happy   **b)** angry   **c)** wealthy   **d)** kind

_____ 43. **plausible**   **a)** unbelievable   **b)** avoidable   **c)** unknown   **d)** thrifty

_____ 44. **exotic**   **a)** best   **b)** worst   **c)** commonplace   **d)** unusual

_____ 45. **revoke**   **a)** state clearly   **b)** remind   **c)** make effective   **d)** prove

_____ 46. **malicious**   **a)** kindly   **b)** smelly   **c)** ordinary   **d)** small

_____ 47. **recede**   **a)** prove   **b)** destroy   **c)** change   **d)** advance

_____ 48. **provoke**   **a)** forget   **b)** speak   **c)** rebuild   **d)** calm

_____ 49. **indulgent**   **a)** disappointed   **b)** humorous   **c)** useful   **d)** strict

_____ 50. **impulsive**   **a)** cautious   **b)** shy   **c)** smart   **d)** impatient

Score   (Number correct) _____   x 2 = _____ %

Enter your score above and in the vocabulary performance chart on the inside back cover of the book.

UNIT THREE: Test 4

Each item below starts with a pair of words in CAPITAL LETTERS. For each item, figure out the relationship between these two words. Then decide which of the choices (*a*, *b*, *c*, or *d*) expresses a similar relationship. Write the letter of your choice on the answer line.

_____ 1. ENDEAVOR : SUCCEED ::
   a. know : fail
   c. compete : win
   b. attack : defend
   d. grow : shrink

_____ 2. INDIGNANT : ANGRY ::
   a. sorrowful : sad
   c. regretful : satisfied
   b. hungry : thirsty
   d. worried : confident

_____ 3. INEVITABLE : DEATH ::
   a. predictable : expected
   c. believable : doubtful
   b. unlucky : guess
   d. unforeseen : accident

_____ 4. PATRON : RESTAURANT ::
   a. client: lawyer
   c. employee : worker
   b. child : adult
   d. chairperson : committee

_____ 5. ADAPT : CLIMATE ::
   a. lose : discovery
   c. adjust : new job
   b. admire : criminal
   d. admit : denial

_____ 6. EXILE : HOMELAND ::
   a. engagement : wedding
   c. divorce : spouse
   b. health : recovery
   d. employment : career

_____ 7. RECEDE : MOVE BACK ::
   a. sit : move around
   c. descend : move up
   b. climb : move sideways
   d. advance : move forward

_____ 8. RITUAL : BAPTISM ::
   a. appliance : dishwasher
   c. dinner : birthday cake
   b. tradition : cloning
   d. superstition : voting

_____ 9. EXOTIC : LOCAL ::
   a. handmade : designed
   c. homegrown : planted
   b. foreign : automobiles
   d. fake : real

_____ 10. IMPULSIVE : UNPREDICTABLE ::
   a. first : last
   c. well-organized : wealthy
   b. fearful : frightened
   d. private : well-known

(Continues on next page)

_____ 11. INDIFFERENT : CONCERNED ::

    a. calm : anxious   b. confident : certain
    c. worried : nervous   d. uninterested : bored

_____ 12. MEDIOCRE : AVERAGE ::

    a. good : best   b. poor : below average
    c. bad : worst   d. average : worse

_____ 13. AFFIRM : DENY ::

    a. state : swear   b. gather : scatter
    c. promise : keep   d. disagree : disprove

_____ 14. IMMUNITY : VACCINATION ::

    a. work : vacation   b. relief : disappointment
    c. knowledge : education   d. tiredness : rest

_____ 15. IMPAIR : DESTROY ::

    a. improve : make perfect   b. want : dislike
    c. strengthen : weaken   d. damage : build

_____ 16. QUERY : ANSWER ::

    a. wed : career   c. speak : sentence
    b. sleep : dinner   d. invite : response

_____ 17. PROVOKE : CALM ::

    a. delay : postpone   b. discourage : stop
    c. recognize : friendship   d. forbid : allow

_____ 18. REPRIMAND : LAZY WORKER ::

    a. praise : noisy neighbor   b. compliment : mugger
    c. thanks: rude store clerk   d. scolding : disobedient child

_____ 19. SKEPTICAL : LIAR ::

    a. admiring : cheater   b. pleased : driver
    c. fearful : killer   d. confused : comedian

_____ 20. STEREOTYPE : IMAGE ::

    a. fact : falsehood   b. opinion : view
    c. reality : dream   d. wish : fear

Score (Number correct) _____ x 5 = _____ %

Enter your score above and in the vocabulary performance chart on the inside back cover of the book.

Unit Four

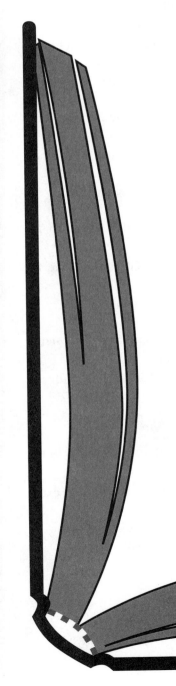

Chapter 16

consequence	simultaneous
destiny	strategy
detain	tedious
diminish	transaction
procrastinate	vital

Chapter 17

discriminate	site
dismal	subside
dispense	summon
profound	theoretical
severity	vocation

Chapter 18

data	morbid
inept	obstinate
innate	parallel
intervene	perceptive
lament	sedate

Chapter 19

confirm	submit
deceptive	susceptible
defy	transmit
restrain	valid
seclusion	vigorous

Chapter 20

accelerate	comparable
adverse	competent
advocate	consecutive
audible	conspicuous
coherent	deteriorate

16

consequence	simultaneous
destiny	strategy
detain	tedious
diminish	transaction
procrastinate	vital

Ten Words in Context

In the space provided, write the letter of the meaning closest to that of each **boldfaced** word. Use the context of the sentences to help you figure out each word's meaning.

1 **consequence**
(kŏn′sĭ-kwĕns)
-noun

- As a **consequence** of her heavy spending at the mall, Lily was short of cash until her next paycheck.
- Small children reach for hot things and sharp objects because they don't know the **consequences** of such actions.

___ *Consequence* means   a. an effect.   b. a cause.   c. a rule.

2 **destiny**
(dĕs′tə-nē)
-noun

- Believing in fate, the soldier wondered if his **destiny** was to die in the coming battle.
- Marc believes that he and Debbie were born for each other and that it was their **destiny** to meet.

___ *Destiny* means   a. a habit.   b. a fate.   c. a hope.

3 **detain**
(dĭ-tān′)
-verb

- Paul's history teacher **detained** him after class to speak privately about his surprisingly low grade on the test.
- **Detained** at home by a friend in urgent need of advice, Gloria was late for work.

___ *Detain* means   a. to delay.   b. to leave.   c. to avoid.

4 **diminish**
(dĭ-mĭn′ĭsh)
-verb

- After Mother yelled, "Turn that thing down!" the sound from the stereo **diminished** from a roar to a soft hum.
- I waited for my anger to **diminish** before discussing the problem with my boss.

___ *Diminish* means   a. to grow.   b. to remain.   c. to become less.

5 **procrastinate**
(prō-krăs′tə-nāt′)
-verb

- Morgan **procrastinated** so long that when she finally returned the dress to the store, it was too late for a refund.
- I can't **procrastinate** any longer. I must study tonight because the final exam is tomorrow morning.

___ *Procrastinate* means   a. to do something efficiently.   b. to remember something.   c. to put off doing something.

6 **simultaneous**
(sī′məl-tā′nē-əs)
-adjective

- In a fair race, all starts must be **simultaneous**.
- Lightning and thunder don't seem to be **simultaneous**—we see the lightning before we hear the thunder.

___ *Simultaneous* means   a. similar.   b. happening at the same time.   c. delayed.

7 strategy
(străt′ə-jē)
-*noun*

- The best **strategy** for teaching children manners is for adults to use good manners themselves.
- The general's **strategy** was to surround the enemy troops during the night.

___ *Strategy* means   a. a reason.   b. a place.   c. a plan.

8 tedious
(tē′dē-əs)
-*adjective*

- **Tedious** chores, like washing dishes, are less boring if you do them while listening to the radio or talking with a friend.
- John found the homework assignment very **tedious**; the questions were dull and repetitious.

___ *Tedious* means   a. uninteresting.   b. serious.   c. unnecessary.

9 transaction
(trăn-săk′shən)
-*noun*

- **Transactions** at flea markets often involve bargaining.
- Among some business people, a **transaction** is concluded with a handshake. These business deals are never put in writing.

___ *Transaction* means   a. a mood.   b. a business interaction.   c. an instruction.

10 vital
(vīt′l)
-*adjective*

- Water is **vital** to the survival of all living things. For example, people who stop drinking liquids will die in just a few days.
- For Teresa to pass her math course, it is **vital** that she pass the final exam.

___ *Vital* means   a. unimportant.   b. essential.   c. not harmful.

Matching Words with Definitions

Following are definitions of the ten words. Clearly write or print each word next to its definition. The sentences above and on the previous page will help you decide on the meaning of each word.

1. _____   Happening or done at the same time

2. _____   To lessen; decrease

3. _____   A method; overall plan

4. _____   A result

5. _____   A business deal or action; exchange of money, goods, or services

6. _____   Necessary; extremely important

7. _____   Boring; uninteresting because of great length, slowness, or repetition

8. _____   To delay; keep from continuing

9. _____   To put off doing something until later

10. _____   Something bound to happen to someone; fate

CAUTION: Do not go any further until you are sure the above answers are correct. Then you can use the definitions to help you in the following practices. Your goal is eventually to know the words well enough so that you don't need to check the definitions at all.

➤ *Sentence Check 1*

Using the answer line provided, complete each item below with the correct word from the box. Use each word once.

a. **consequence**	b. **destiny**	c. **detain**	d. **diminish**	e. **procrastinate**
f. **simultaneous**	g. **strategy**	h. **tedious**	i. **transaction**	j. **vital**

_____ 1. The ___ at the checkout counter was delayed by an incorrect price label.

_____ 2. The afternoon sunshine caused the snowman's height to ___ from six feet to three.

_____ 3. To ___ is to follow the old saying "Never do today what you can put off until tomorrow."

_____ 4. As a ___ of his staying out too late, Wilson wasn't allowed out for a week.

_____ 5. The dancers' movements were meant to be ___. But when the ballerina leaped, her partner failed to move in time to catch her.

_____ 6. Helen's chess ___ is to make her moves so quickly that her opponent believes she's an expert.

_____ 7. Ryan felt it was his wife's ___ to die in the fire. He refused to believe her death was meaningless.

_____ 8. The secret agent paid for information he thought was ___ to our national safety, but he had been tricked into buying useless knowledge.

_____ 9. "If my science teacher didn't ___ us past the bell every day, I wouldn't be late for my next class," explained George.

_____ 10. To make raking autumn leaves less ___, my sister and I took turns jumping into the newly created piles.

NOTE: Now check your answers to these questions by turning to page 130. Going over the answers carefully will help you prepare for the next two practices, for which answers are not given.

➤ *Sentence Check 2*

Using the answer lines provided, complete each item below with **two** words from the box. Use each word once.

_____
_____ 1–2. Before the tug-of-war started, the blue team decided on a ___: each time the captain shouted "Go!" all team members would give hard ___ pulls.

_____
_____ 3–4. "I'm sorry to ___ you," the salesman said, "but a ___ involving payment with a personal check takes longer than a cash purchase."

_____
_____ 5–6. The ___ of poor nutrition is illness. In addition to enough exercise and sleep, a balanced diet is ___ for health.

_____   7–8. Unfortunately, it doesn't help to ___ in paying your bills—putting them
_____   off doesn't make them ___ or disappear. In fact, late payers not only
                                 impair° their credit ratings; they end up paying more because of late
                                 charges and interest payments.

_____   9–10. "This job is so ___ that I'm afraid I'll die of boredom," said the file
_____   clerk. "Is it my ___ to put things in alphabetical order for the rest of my
                                 life?"

➤ *Final Check:* **Procrastinator**

Here is a final opportunity for you to strengthen your knowledge of the ten words. First read the following
selection carefully. Then fill in each blank with a word from the box at the top of the previous page.
(Context clues will help you figure out which word goes in which blank.) Use each word once.

One of these days there is going to be a "new me": I will no longer (1) _Pro_____ .

I'm making this my New Year's resolution. Well, yes, I concede° that it's March and I still haven't

acted. I was going to make this resolution in January, but all that Christmas shopping and cookie

baking (2) _de_____(e)d me. In February I figured out a (3) _Str_____

to help me stop putting things off, and I'll get around to it soon because I know it's

(4) _Vit_____ for me to change my ways. My problem is that some jobs are

so (5)_____ that just thinking of them makes me want to yawn. But I

know that the (6)_____ of putting things off is that nothing actually gets

done. And once I get started on my New Year's resolution, a new me will emerge°. My tendency

to delay things will surely gradually (7)_____. I'll finish every household

project and financial (8)_____ that I start. A good tactic° would be to

make a list of activities that can be done (9)_____ly, such as sewing while

watching TV, or cleaning my junk drawer and talking to my mother on the phone at the same time.

I'd make a list now if I could just find a pen. I was going to buy pens yesterday, but I figured I'd be

at the mall on Friday, so why make a special trip? I'll make the list later. Oh well, maybe it's just

my (10)_____ to put things off. If it's inevitable°, why fight it?

Scores	Sentence Check 2 _____%	Final Check _____%

Enter your scores above and in the vocabulary performance chart on the inside back cover of the book.

CHAPTER
17

discriminate	site
dismal	subside
dispense	summon
profound	theoretical
severity	vocation

Ten Words in Context

In the space provided, write the letter of the meaning closest to that of each **boldfaced** word. Use the context of the sentences to help you figure out each word's meaning.

1 discriminate
(dĭ-skrĭm′ə-nāt′)
-verb

- It's easy to **discriminate** between canned and fresh vegetables—fresh vegetables taste much better.
- Tests show that women tend to **discriminate** among colors better than men. Cherry red, cranberry red, and purplish red are all simply dark red to many men.

___ *Discriminate* means   a. to tell the difference.   b. to become confused.   c. to make an error.

2 dismal
(dĭz′məl)
-adjective

- Kyle was disappointed by the **dismal** news that his knee injury would keep him out of college for a whole semester.
- "It is a **dismal** rainy day," Mona told her disappointed children. "But we don't have to cancel the picnic—we can have it on the kitchen floor."

___ *Dismal* means   a. welcome.   b. lengthy.   c. gloomy.

3 dispense
(dĭ-spĕns′)
-verb

- The broken soda machine **dispensed** either a cup or soda, but not both together.
- Restroom soap holders that are supposed to **dispense** liquid soap at each push seem to be empty most of the time.

___ *Dispense* means   a. to pay.   b. to give out.   c. to do without.

4 profound
(prə-found′)
-adjective

- The death of a spouse can cause **profound** depression that, in some cases, can even lead to the death of the partner.
- Ever since her stepfather insulted her mother, Serena has had a **profound** hatred of him.

___ *Profound* means   a. deep.   b. mild.   c. accidental.

5 severity
(sə-vĕr′ə-tē)
-noun

- The **severity** of the fire could be seen in the burned, smoking ruins of the once beautiful building.
- Mark believes the **severity** of his punishment was too great. A hundred hours of weekend trash cleanup seemed too harsh a penalty for throwing two Coke cans onto the highway.

___ *Severity* means   a. gentleness.   b. intensity.   c. a cause.

6 site
(sīt)
-noun

- The oldest private home in the New England town was named a historical **site**.
- Wounded Knee, South Dakota, is the **site** of a conflict between the federal government and the Sioux Indians in 1973.

___ *Site* means   a. a state.   b. a fact.   c. a place.

7 subside
(səb-sīd′)
-verb

- When I'm really furious, a walk around the block makes the anger **subside**.
- Consuela sat in her car until the storm **subsided**. Then she dashed up the sidewalk and into school.

__ *Subside* means
  a. to begin.
  b. to lessen.
  c. to increase.

8 summon
(sŭm′ən)
-verb

- When the king couldn't sleep, he would **summon** the court clown to come and entertain him.
- The principal liked to **summon** troublesome students to his office by announcing their names over the loudspeaker.

__ *Summon* means
  a. to order.
  b. to see.
  c. to allow.

9 theoretical
(thē′ə-rĕt′ĭ-kəl)
-adjective

- At first, Cruz enjoyed simply looking through his telescope. However, when questions occurred to him, he began to read **theoretical** explanations of what he was seeing.
- The teacher explained the **theoretical** basis for the chemistry experiment so the class would understand why it worked as it did.

__ *Theoretical* means
  a. about action.
  b. about theory.
  c. only imagined.

10 vocation
(vō-kā′shən)
-noun

- Raising collies was just a hobby for Louise. Her **vocation** was library science.
- If you can't decide on a career, you might wish to take a test that reveals which **vocations** you're suited for.

__ *Vocation* means
  a. recreation.
  b. an activity.
  c. an occupation.

Matching Words with Definitions

Following are definitions of the ten words. Clearly write or print each word next to its definition. The sentences above and on the previous page will help you decide on the meaning of each word.

1. _____ Deeply felt

2. _____ To see differences; distinguish

3. _____ The past, present, or future location of a building or buildings or an event

4. _____ A profession or occupation

5. _____ About or based on theory (as opposed to practice or practical use)

6. _____ Gloomy; cheerless; depressing

7. _____ To send for; order to come

8. _____ To give out in portions or amounts

9. _____ The condition or quality of being severe; harshness; intensity; seriousness

10. _____ To become less active; calm down; decrease

CAUTION: Do not go any further until you are sure the above answers are correct. Then you can use the definitions to help you in the following practices. Your goal is eventually to know the words well enough so that you don't need to check the definitions at all.

➤ *Sentence Check 1*

Using the answer line provided, complete each item below with the correct word from the box. Use each word once.

a. **discriminate**	b. **dismal**	c. **dispense**	d. **profound**	e. **severity**
f. **site**	g. **subside**	h. **summon**	i. **theoretical**	j. **vocation**

_____ 1. Since the alligator and the crocodile look so much alike, most people cannot ___ between them.

_____ 2. Growing up with poverty gave Timika a ___ desire to help others in need.

_____ 3. Near the shore, the waves were enormous, but as we rowed out into open water, they began to ___.

_____ 4. I thought I was in trouble when my boss ___(e)d me to her office—until she told me I was getting a raise.

_____ 5. Among the most dangerous ___s are deep-sea diving, mining, and construction.

_____ 6. This room is too ___. It needs a party to brighten it up.

_____ 7. Do you think food machines at public schools should ___ only nutritious foods, such as fruit and juices?

_____ 8. Medication should match the ___ of a problem. A powerful painkiller isn't needed for a hangnail.

_____ 9. I can use the math formulas, but I don't understand the ___ basis for them.

_____ 10. Although the ___ where the hiker claimed a spaceship had landed was burned, no one believed him.

NOTE: Now check your answers to these questions by turning to page 130. Going over the answers carefully will help you prepare for the next two practices, for which answers are not given.

➤ *Sentence Check 2*

Using the answer lines provided, complete each item below with **two** words from the box. Use each word once.

_____
_____ 1–2. My visit to the school for learning-disabled children had a ___ effect on me—it changed my career plans. I was going to be a nurse, but that day I decided my ___ would be in special education.

_____
_____ 3–4. It is hard to convey° the terror one feels in seeing someone get hit by a car. It was not until I was ten miles away from the ___ of the accident that my shaking began to ___.

_____   5–6. The movie was meant to be a dark comedy, but I found it to be ___. I
_____   often couldn't ___ between lines in the dialog° that were meant to be
                              funny and lines that were just depressing.

_____   7–8. If you have a question about the principles of this music, we will have
_____   to ___ Mr. Burns from his office. A notable° author of music textbooks,
                              he has studied music for years. I can play the music, but I have no ___
                              knowledge.

_____   9–10. Some hospitals now allow patients to judge the ___ of their own pain
_____   and to ___ small amounts of medication to themselves as necessary.

➤ *Final Check:* A Change in View

Here is a final opportunity for you to strengthen your knowledge of the ten words. First read the following
selection carefully. Then fill in each blank with a word from the box at the top of the previous page.
(Context clues will help you figure out which word goes in which blank.) Use each word once.

What an education I got yesterday! I am studying to be a nurse. Part of my preparation for this

(1)_____ is (2)_____ and part is practical experience.

Yesterday, after weeks of studying about mental illness in textbooks, I began my training in a

mental hospital. Influenced by the movie stereotype° of such hospitals as being full of zombies

and wild people, I was scared. I imagined dark, (3)_____ rooms where people

sat staring and drooling. I pictured screaming, sadistic° patients trying to hurt me so badly that I

would have to (4)_____ the guards. But yesterday my view of mental

hospitals and their patients went through a (5)_____ change. First of all, the

(6)_____ of the hospital is at the edge of a lovely small town, and its grounds

are green and neat. When I arrived there, I was brought to a big, cheerful room filled with patients

whose morale° was high. They were talking, doing craft projects, or playing Ping-Pong or cards.

I spoke to one patient. She seemed like a nice, normal person who happened to have problems.

She reminisced° about the time she first came to the hospital, when the (7)_____

of her illness had been much greater. At that time, she could not always (8)_____

between what was real and what she imagined. Like many patients, she was often upset and

confused. But the doctors put her on medicine, which the nurses still (9)_____

three times a day. The medicine, as well as talks with the doctors, nurses, and other patients, has

helped make her symptoms (10)_____. Perhaps our conversation was helpful

to her; I know it helped me. Now I'm thinking about working in the mental health field after I get

my nursing degree.

> *Scores*   Sentence Check 2 _____%   Final Check _____%

Enter your scores above and in the vocabulary performance chart on the inside back cover of the book.

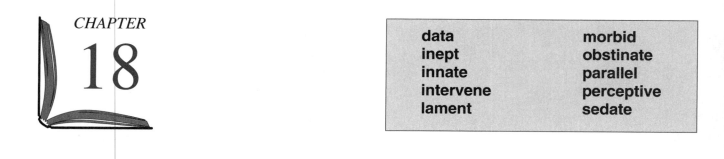

data	morbid
inept	obstinate
innate	parallel
intervene	parallel
lament	perceptive
	sedate

Ten Words in Context

In the space provided, write the letter of the meaning closest to that of each **boldfaced** word. Use the context of the sentences to help you figure out each word's meaning.

1 **data**
(dā′tə)
-*noun*

- Marva considers the available **data** on a car—including its fuel economy, safety, and repair record—before deciding whether to buy it.
- Jane Goodall collected important **data** on chimpanzees by observing them in the wild.

___ *Data* means   a. dates.   b. information.   c. goals.

2 **inept**
(ĭn-ĕpt′)
-*adjective*

- I am so **inept** at carpentry that in my hand, a hammer is a dangerous weapon.
- Since the actress was **inept** at playing comic characters, she decided to try out only for dramatic roles.

___ *Inept* means   a. effective.   b. unskilled.   c. calm.

3 **innate**
(ĭ-nāt′)
-*adjective*

- Rick's musical ability must be **innate**. Even as a young child, he could play the piano by ear and make up his own tunes.
- Psychologists try to learn which of our abilities and interests are **innate** and which of them we gain through experience.

___ *Innate* means   a. inherited.   b. worthwhile.   c. learned through experience.

4 **intervene**
(ĭn′tər-vēn′)
-*verb*

- The two boxers would have killed each other if the referee hadn't finally **intervened**.
- When my parents argue, I get out of the way rather than trying to **intervene**.

___ *Intervene* means   a. to leave.   b. to pass through.   c. to come between.

5 **lament**
(lə-mĕnt′)
-*verb*

- When her mother died, Evelyn **lamented** her passing for weeks, crying every day.
- Blues songs **lament** loneliness, sadness, and the hardships of life, rather than celebrating happy situations.

___ *Lament* means   a. to mourn.   b. to doubt.   c. to disturb.

6 **morbid**
(môr′bĭd)
-*adjective*

- Great comedians can turn a topic as **morbid** as murder into a source of laughter.
- On Halloween, sweet little Nickie chose a **morbid** costume—a disgusting-looking monster with a "bloody" hand and hatchet.

___ *Morbid* means   a. horrible.   b. convenient.   c. boring.

7 obstinate
(ŏb′stə-nĭt)
-adjective

- No matter how much I urged him, Andrew remained **obstinate**—he refused to make up with Lamar, who was once his best friend.
- My father is usually very **obstinate**, but not with his sister, who is even more stubborn than he is.

__ *Obstinate* means   a. lazy.   b. dishonest.   c. stubborn.

8 parallel
(păr′ə-lĕl′)
-adjective

- To make the stripes he was painting **parallel**, Alexei measured to be sure there were exactly three inches between them at the top, middle, and bottom.
- **Parallel** lines run alongside each other but never meet.

__ *Parallel* means   a. clear.   b. apart an equal distance at every point.   c. going up and down.

9 perceptive
(pər-sĕp′tĭv)
-adjective

- Children are more **perceptive** than many people think. They can usually sense their parents' moods and know whether or not it is a good time to ask for something.
- Professor Banks is very **perceptive**. She always seems to know which of her students are under unusual stress.

__ *Perceptive* means   a. detached.   b. aware.   c. selfish.

10 sedate
(sĭ-dāt′)
-adjective

- While the officer wrote out the ticket, Beverly remained **sedate**, and then she even wished him a pleasant day. But after he left, she pounded the steering wheel and screamed, "Why me!?"
- An experienced surgeon, Dr. Greenbaum remains **sedate** even in an emergency, performing the most complicated operations with complete calm.

__ *Sedate* means   a. angry.   b. doubtful.   c. calm.

Matching Words with Definitions

Following are definitions of the ten words. Clearly write or print each word next to its definition. The sentences above and on the previous page will help you decide on the meaning of each word.

1. _____   To come between in order to influence an action, an argument, etc.

2. _____   Calm and dignified; serious and unemotional

3. _____   The same distance apart at every point

4. _____   Understanding and insightful; observant; aware

5. _____   Information gathered for a study or a decision

6. _____   Possessed at birth; inborn

7. _____   To express sorrow for or about; mourn for

8. _____   Shocking and disgusting; horrible; gruesome

9. _____   Clumsy; unskillful

10. _____   Stubborn

CAUTION: Do not go any further until you are sure the above answers are correct. Then you can use the definitions to help you in the following practices. Your goal is eventually to know the words well enough so that you don't need to check the definitions at all.

➤ *Sentence Check 1*

Using the answer line provided, complete each item below with the correct word from the box. Use each word once.

a. **data**	b. **inept**	c. **innate**	d. **intervene**	e. **lament**
f. **morbid**	g. **obstinate**	h. **parallel**	i. **perceptive**	j. **sedate**

_____ 1. For his psychology experiment, Rudy is gathering ___ to show which memory aids work best for students.

_____ 2. I'm so ___ at bowling that I usually roll the ball straight into the gutter.

_____ 3. The child had nightmares after he listened to a(n) ___ story about Dracula that was full of attacks by vampires.

_____ 4. While my dog gets excited easily, my cat remains ___ even when everyone around her is in a whirl of activity.

_____ 5. When you frame a picture, the picture's edges should be ___ to those of the frame, not dipping down or slanting up.

_____ 6. Kwan is so ___ that she often correctly judges a person's character after a brief conversation.

_____ 7. When children get into a fight, it is sometimes best not to ___, but to let them work it out themselves.

_____ 8. Shawna tried to persuade her son to join the family for dinner, but he was ___, refusing to leave his room no matter what she said.

_____ 9. People all over the United States ___(e)d the death of Martin Luther King, who is now honored with a national holiday on his birthday.

_____ 10. Richard's gift for fixing machines seems ___. Even as a child, he could take one look at a broken machine and know what was wrong with it.

NOTE: Now check your answers to these questions by turning to page 130. Going over the answers carefully will help you prepare for the next two practices, for which answers are not given.

➤ *Sentence Check 2*

Using the answer lines provided, complete each item below with **two** words from the box. Use each word once.

_____
_____ 1–2. As a child, Calvin was ___, rarely excited or upset. As a teenager, however, he is often angry and ___—so stubborn that he hates to change his mind. We hope that after adolescence, he'll revert° to being calm again.

_____
_____ 3–4. Angie loves shocking films. She has seen every ___ horror movie ever made and even collects ___ about the films—dates, actors, directors, etc.

_____ 5–6. Jason's math ability must be ___. By age 2 he could add and subtract,
_____   and by 7 he understood the concept that two ___ lines can't meet no
                                  matter how long they are.

_____ 7–8. "I ___ the passing of the days when employees did their jobs right," the
_____   shop owner complained. "Today, workers not only are ___ but do
                                  nothing to improve their skills."

_____ 9–10. A good marriage counselor is ___ enough to understand both the
_____   husband's and the wife's points of view. And rather than ___ in the
                                   couple's arguments, the counselor helps them learn strategies° for
                                   solving their problems themselves.

➤ *Final Check:* **Family Differences**

Here is a final opportunity for you to strengthen your knowledge of the ten words. First read the following
selection carefully. Then fill in each blank with a word from the box at the top of the previous page.
(Context clues will help you figure out which word goes in which blank.) Use each word once.

I am always amazed at how different all of my brothers and sisters are. Sheila, who succeeds
at everything she tries, simply has no patience with the rest of us. She thinks we are
(1)_____ at everything and that it's up to her to (2)_____ in
what we do so that things will be done the right way—her way. Jack, on the other hand, is very
(3)_____. He doesn't let anything bother him, and so he rarely loses his temper
and is quite indulgent° of the desires of others. Chris is the one who never gives in. As a baby, he
was already so (4)_____ that he would spit food he didn't like right at my
mother. Daisy, the most social, likes people and seems to have a(n) (5)_____
ability to make them feel good. She has always been very (6)_____, knowing
just what mood others were in and what they might need. Frank is the weird one. He has always
been attracted by unusual activities. While the rest of us kids would be riding bikes or jumping
ropes, he would be doing something (7)_____, like holding a funeral for a
dead frog or bird or snake. He got mad at us whenever we failed to (8)_____ a
death as much as he did. Betty has the quickest mind of us all. When she was just 4, she told my
dad, "Those two shelves aren't (9)_____—they are farther apart on the left
than on the right." By age 6, she was collecting (10)_____ for a book she was
writing on insects. Also inventive, Betty has devised° various gadgets around our house, including
a doorbell for our dog. Yes, my brothers and sisters are all different. They may be strange at times,
but they're never boring.

Scores	Sentence Check 2 _____%	Final Check _____%

Enter your scores above and in the vocabulary performance chart on the inside back cover of the book.

confirm	submit
deceptive	susceptible
defy	transmit
restrain	valid
seclusion	vigorous

Ten Words in Context

In the space provided, write the letter of the meaning closest to that of each **boldfaced** word. Use the context of the sentences to help you figure out each word's meaning.

1 confirm
(kən-fûrm′)
-verb

- Mr. Smith was released by the police when someone **confirmed** his statement that he had been out of town the day of the murder.
- "Yes, it's true," the manager said, **confirming** the report that his star player had asked to be traded to another team.

___ *Confirm* means   a. to deny.   b. to support.   c. to ignore.

2 deceptive
(dĭ-sĕp′tĭv)
-adjective

- The seeming ease with which Nadia plays the piano is **deceptive**. Actually, she practices four hours each day.
- After stealing the radio, Meg remained silent while another student was wrongly accused. Her silence was as **deceptive** as an outright lie.

___ *Deceptive* means   a. modest.   b. flexible.   c. misleading.

3 defy
(dĭ-fī′)
-verb

- The automotive plant workers voted to **defy** the company and go on strike.
- After being forbidden to go out three evenings in a row, Ted **defied** his parents by walking right out the front door.

___ *Defy* means   a. to oppose.   b. to support.   c. to learn from.

4 restrain
(rĭ-strān′)
-verb

- I **restrained** myself from laughing when my brother made a funny face while Uncle William told us—yet again—the story of his operation. I certainly did not want to hurt Uncle Will's feelings.
- Larry was so angry that we had to **restrain** him by force from punching Neal.

___ *Restrain* means   a. to forgive.   b. to prevent.   c. to train.

5 seclusion
(sĭ-kloo′zhən)
-noun

- The **seclusion** of the mountain cabin started to bother Veronica. She missed the city and being with other people.
- I work best in **seclusion**, where no one can interrupt the flow of my thoughts.

___ *Seclusion* means   a. isolation.   b. crowding.   c. relaxation.

6 submit
(səb-mĭt′)
-verb

- After bucking wildly for several minutes, the horse calmed down and **submitted** to the rider.
- For reasons of security, travelers must **submit** to having their luggage inspected at airports.

___ *Submit* means   a. to object.   b. to admit.   c. to give in.

7 susceptible
(sə-sĕp′tə-bəl)
-*adjective*

- Lina is so **susceptible** to blushing that she turns away whenever she is embarrassed so that no one will see her face change color.
- People who smoke are more **susceptible** to colds than others.

__ *Susceptible* means   a. happy about.   b. likely to be affected with.   c. attracted by.

8 transmit
(trăns-mĭt′)
-*verb*

- Emergency messages were **transmitted** over all the city's radio stations.
- Before the microscope was invented, no one knew that a person could **transmit** a disease to someone else through "invisible" germs.

__ *Transmit* means   a. to pass along.   b. to check.   c. to lose.

9 valid
(văl′ĭd)
-*adjective*

- The research study was not **valid** because much of the "evidence" had been made up by the researcher.
- "Your accusation that I'm not responsible isn't **valid**," Myra told her father. "I've done all my homework already and even cleaned the living room."

__ *Valid* means   a. obvious.   b. well-supported.   c. wrong.

10 vigorous
(vĭg′ər-əs)
-*adjective*

- My eighty-year-old grandmother is still **vigorous** enough to walk five miles every day.
- The best instructors have **vigorous** teaching styles, lively enough to make any lesson interesting.

__ *Vigorous* means   a. strict.   b. quiet.   c. energetic.

Matching Words with Definitions

Following are definitions of the ten words. Clearly write or print each word next to its definition. The sentences above and on the previous page will help you decide on the meaning of each word.

1. _____   The condition of being apart or far from others

2. _____   Likely to be affected with or influenced; likely to be infected

3. _____   Misleading; intended or intending to deceive

4. _____   To boldly oppose; openly resist; stand up

5. _____   To support; show the truth of

6. _____   Firmly based on facts or logic; logical; based on good reasons

7. _____   Lively; energetic

8. _____   To give in to another's authority or will; yield

9. _____   To communicate; pass or spread (information, an illness, etc.)

10. _____   To hold back from action

CAUTION: Do not go any further until you are sure the above answers are correct. Then you can use the definitions to help you in the following practices. Your goal is eventually to know the words well enough so that you don't need to check the definitions at all.

➤ *Sentence Check 1*

Using the answer line provided, complete each item below with the correct word from the box. Use each word once.

a. **confirm**	b. **deceptive**	c. **defy**	d. **restrain**	e. **seclusion**
f. **submit**	g. **susceptible**	h. **transmit**	i. **valid**	j. **vigorous**

_____ 1. I gave the bottle such a ___ shake that it leaked Russian dressing all over my hands.

_____ 2. The dinosaur theory seemed ___ because all the available evidence supported it.

_____ 3. I don't go to the beach because I'm so ___ to sunburn.

_____ 4. At the party, Nick ___(ed) the rumor that he was engaged when he introduced his date as his fiancée.

_____ 5. In prison, the criminal had to ___ to more rules than he had ever thought possible.

_____ 6. The widow stayed in ___ for a period of mourning, not seeing visitors or going to any social events.

_____ 7. The little boy tried to___ his big dog from chasing a car, but he could not hold the dog back.

_____ 8. "Looks can be ___," Ray's big brother warned. "Wendy may have a cute, childish face, but she's far from sweet."

_____ 9. To save on long-distance telephone charges, Tia decided to ___ the news about the baby's birth by e-mail.

_____ 10. The daring thief liked to openly ___ the police by leaving this note at the scene of the crime: "Love and kisses from 'The Uncatchable One.'"

NOTE: Now check your answers to these questions by turning to page 130. Going over the answers carefully will help you prepare for the next two practices, for which answers are not given.

➤ *Sentence Check 2*

Using the answer lines provided, complete each item below with **two** words from the box. Use each word once.

_____
_____ 1–2. The police made a ___ effort to ___ the angry mob from pushing through the gates. However, the mob prevailed° and pushed the gates open wide.

_____
_____ 3–4. Children who must ___ to overly strict rules often openly ___ their parents when they get older.

_____
_____ 5–6. Buddy is so ___ to ear infections that he is never surprised to hear the doctor ___ his suspicion that he has yet another one.

_____   7–8. The prisoners of war were kept in ___ for three months except for
_____   Christmas Day, when they were permitted to see others and to ___
                           messages to their families over a radio.

_____   9–10. The title of the magazine article—"Miracle Weight Loss"—was ___. It
_____   suggested that there is a magical way to lose weight, but such a claim
                           isn't ___—the facts show otherwise.

➤ *Final Check:* Chicken Pox

Here is a final opportunity for you to strengthen your knowledge of the ten words. First read the following selection carefully. Then fill in each blank with a word from the box at the top of the previous page. (Context clues will help you figure out which word goes in which blank.) Use each word once.

I remember the day my brother Danny dragged himself home from third grade and complained, "Mommy, I don't feel too good." My mother took one look at my usually (1)_____ brother, yelled "Aargh!" and flew up the stairs with him. The other four of us ran after them, demanding to know what deadly disease he had. "Get away!" my mother cried. "It's chicken pox. He has to stay in (2)_____ until all his spots are gone."

Poor Danny had to (3)_____ to having his spots checked by all the other mothers in the neighborhood. "Spots can be (4)_____," one woman explained. "They might have been measles, but I have to (5)_____ your mother's conclusion. These are definitely chicken pox." Another mother brought a photo from a medical book that verified° the diagnosis of chicken pox.

After the women left, my mother said firmly, "None of you is to set foot in Danny's room for at least seven days. I don't want him to (6)_____ this disease to you. I don't think I could survive having the other four of you sick all at once."

Then I came to an interesting conclusion: if my mother's claim that Danny's spots would last at least a week was (7)_____, that meant he would get out of school for a week. I was filled with jealousy. Still, I didn't want to openly (8)_____ my mother, so I didn't go to Danny's room during the daylight hours. However, unable to (9)_____ myself, I crawled into bed with him each night, tempted by the promise of a one-week vacation.

Although my mother says I purposely set out to destroy her sanity, the situation wasn't all that drastic°. The four of us didn't get sick simultaneously°. Instead, my sisters got sick two weeks after I did. Today, we are no longer (10)_____ to chicken pox—we all have immunity°. Now, if we want to stay home from school, we'll have to catch something else.

Scores	Sentence Check 2 _____%	Final Check _____%

Enter your scores above and in the vocabulary performance chart on the inside back cover of the book.

CHAPTER

20

accelerate	comparable
adverse	competent
advocate	consecutive
audible	conspicuous
coherent	deteriorate

Ten Words in Context

In the space provided, write the letter of the meaning closest to that of each **boldfaced** word. Use the context of the sentences to help you figure out each word's meaning.

1 accelerate
(ăk-sĕl′ə-rāt′)
-verb

- The sleds began sliding down the hill slowly and then **accelerated** to flying speed.
- Doug's car **accelerated** rapidly, allowing him to catch up with the slowly moving ice-cream truck.

___ *Accelerate* means   a. to go down.   b. to go faster.   c. to hesitate.

2 adverse
(ăd-vûrs′)
-adjective

- Mozart created musical masterpieces in spite of his **adverse** circumstances—illness and debt.
- **Adverse** newspaper reviews persuaded many people not to see the violent new movie.

___ *Adverse* means   a. unknown.   b. unfavorable.   c. unnecessary.

3 advocate
(ăd′və-kĭt)
-noun

- My physician is an **advocate** of using nicotine gum to quit smoking. She says the gum helps people resist cigarettes.
- Our minister is a strong **advocate** of a drug-free America. He often mentions it in his sermons.

___ *Advocate* means   a. a critic.   b. an example.   c. a supporter.

4 audible
(ô′də-bəl)
-adjective

- Dogs, bats, and other animals can hear high-pitched sounds that are not **audible** to humans.
- The argument next door was barely **audible**. So I put a cup on the wall and put my ear to the cup so I could hear better.

___ *Audible* means   a. useful.   b. logical.   c. hearable.

5 coherent
(kō-hîr′ənt)
-adjective

- To be sure that your essay has a **coherent** organization, write an outline first.
- The article about the robbery was not **coherent**. The events were not presented in logical order.

___ *Coherent* means   a. clear.   b. complicated.   c. long.

6 comparable
(kŏm′pər-ə-bəl)
-adjective

- Since the quality of relatively new used cars is often **comparable** to that of brand-new ones, my parents never buy new cars.
- Because the two jobs were **comparable** in challenge, interest, and salary, Santos had trouble deciding which to take.

___ *Comparable* means   a. helpful.   b. close.   c. different.

114

7 competent
(kŏm′pĭ-tənt)
-*adjective*

C

Competent means

- Some secretaries are more **competent** than their bosses. They know more about the business, are better organized, and work much harder.
- To be a **competent** juggler takes a lot of practice.
  - a. honest.
  - b. friendly.
  - c. able.

8 consecutive
(kən-sĕk′yə-tĭv)
-*adjective*

C

Consecutive means

- The reporters would work nights for two **consecutive** weeks, and then they'd work days for a month straight.
- First Vera had the flu. That was immediately followed by strep throat, which was followed by pneumonia. These **consecutive** illnesses kept her out of work for two months.
  - a. minor.
  - b. obvious.
  - c. happening in a row.

9 conspicuous
(kən-spĭk′yōō-əs)
-*adjective*

A

Conspicuous means

- Becky's wide-brimmed red hat is so **conspicuous** that it's impossible not to catch sight of her in a crowd.
- The new skyscraper stands fifty stories high, making it the tallest and thus the most **conspicuous** building in the city's skyline.
  - a. noticeable.
  - b. poor in quality or condition.
  - c. serious.

10 deteriorate
(dĭ-tîr′ē-ə-rāt)
-*verb*

C

Deteriorate means

- Over many years, the abandoned house had **deteriorated** until its walls crumbled and its floorboards rotted.
- Jenny's health continued to **deteriorate** until her classmates started to visit her regularly. Then she began to improve.
  - a. to stay the same.
  - b. to improve.
  - c. to decay.

Matching Words with Definitions

Following are definitions of the ten words. Clearly write or print each word next to its definition. The sentences above and on the previous page will help you decide on the meaning of each word.

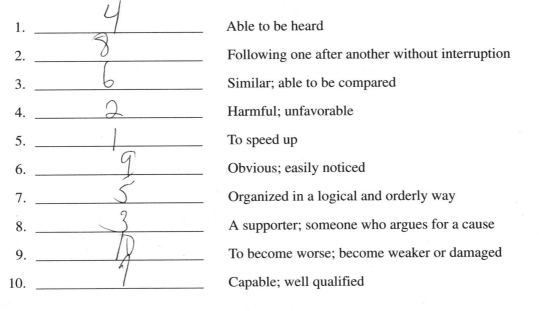

1. _____ 4 _____ Able to be heard

2. _____ 8 _____ Following one after another without interruption

3. _____ 6 _____ Similar; able to be compared

4. _____ 2 _____ Harmful; unfavorable

5. _____ 1 _____ To speed up

6. _____ 9 _____ Obvious; easily noticed

7. _____ 5 _____ Organized in a logical and orderly way

8. _____ 3 _____ A supporter; someone who argues for a cause

9. _____ 10 _____ To become worse; become weaker or damaged

10. _____ 7 _____ Capable; well qualified

CAUTION: Do not go any further until you are sure the above answers are correct. Then you can use the definitions to help you in the following practices. Your goal is eventually to know the words well enough so that you don't need to check the definitions at all.

➤ *Sentence Check 1*

Using the answer line provided, complete each item below with the correct word from the box. Use each word once.

a. accelerate	b. adverse	c. advocate	d. audible	e. coherent
f. comparable	g. competent	h. consecutive	i. conspicuous	j. deteriorate

_____ 1. Dee doesn't like to be _I_, so she sits in the back of the classroom, where few can see her.

_____ 2. Anyone can become a(n) _G_ cook, but few people develop into great chefs.

_____ 3. The weather was bad, and two of the astronauts were sick. Because of these _B_ conditions, the shuttle flight was canceled.

_____ 4. Since I hate pollution, I'm a(n) _C_ of passing laws that limit the amount of pollution in the air.

_____ 5. When the comedian sensed his audience was becoming bored, he _A_d his pace to more jokes per minute.

_____ 6. At the movies, Tina put her arm around Ben and said in a barely _D_ whisper, "I love you. Pass the popcorn."

_____ 7. Ben and Tina's relationship began to _J_ after they had a big fight over money.

_____ 8. People often bring up their own children in a manner that is _F_ to the way they were raised. Thus abused children may become abusing parents.

_____ 9. During her high fever, Celia loudly called out broken words and phrases. She seemed unable to speak in full, _e_ sentences.

_____ 10. There was no break in the summer's heat. Records were set nationwide for the number of _h_ days above ninety degrees.

NOTE: Now check your answers to these questions by turning to page 130. Going over the answers carefully will help you prepare for the next two practices, for which answers are not given.

➤ *Sentence Check 2*

Using the answer lines provided, complete each item below with **two** words from the box. Use each word once.

_____
_____ 1–2. "Has your marriage started to _J_ because of recurring° conflicts?" asked the radio announcer. "If so, you may benefit from the services of Dr. Louis Frank, one of the city's most _F_ and perceptive° marriage counselors."

_____
_____ 3–4. Our neighbors have had parties this week on three _h_ nights—Friday, Saturday, and Sunday. And they played their stereo so loudly that it was _D_ in our bedrooms.

_____ 5-6. The sun has a(n) ___ effect on the skin. It _B_s the aging of the skin, A resulting in more wrinkles at a younger age, and can also cause skin cancer, which can be lethal°.

_____ 7-8. Since the assembly instructions were not ___, we had to figure out ourselves how to put the bike together. Including such poorly written instructions is ___ to including none at all.

_____ 9-10. After driving around a neighborhood for twenty minutes before finding the address we were looking for, we became ___s of ___ house numbers—not ones hidden by shrubs.

➤ Final Check: Walking

Here is a final opportunity for you to strengthen your knowledge of the ten words. First read the following selection carefully. Then fill in each blank with a word from the box at the top of the previous page. (Context clues will help you figure out which word goes in which blank.) Use each word once.

I am a strong (1)_____ of walking rather than jogging. The two activities are in no way (2)_____. Walking is deceptive°; while it seems very relaxing, it nevertheless is vigorous° enough exercise to stimulate° the heart and other muscles. Walking can also be done during all but the most (3)_____ conditions, such as icy sidewalks or a thunderstorm. Walking is also rather easy to learn; most people, in fact, are quite (4)__Component____ at it by their teens (but then they learn to drive, and the ability starts to (5)__Pet____). Moreover, walking is so harmless that one can walk on as many (6)____lt____ days as one wishes. However, jogging jolts the body so much that one cannot do it even two days in a row without causing damage to one's internal organs. In addition, the heavy impact° of joggers' steps makes their fronts and rears shake in such a (7)_____ manner that passersby can't help staring. Walkers, on the other hand, keep their pride. Unlike a runner, a walker needs to (8)_____ only if a growling dog appears nearby. Also, walkers can hold a conversation while walking that is (9)_____ enough to make sense. In contrast, the jogger's brain is too shaken to produce orderly sentences, and the voice is reduced to a barely (10)_____ gasp. Certainly, walking is in every way superior to jogging. In walking, you just pass by. In jogging, you also pass out.

> **Scores**   Sentence Check 2 _____%   Final Check _____%

Enter your scores above and in the vocabulary performance chart on the inside back cover of the book.

UNIT FOUR: Review

The box at the right lists twenty-five words from Unit Four. Using the clues at the bottom of the page, fill in these words to complete the puzzle that follows.

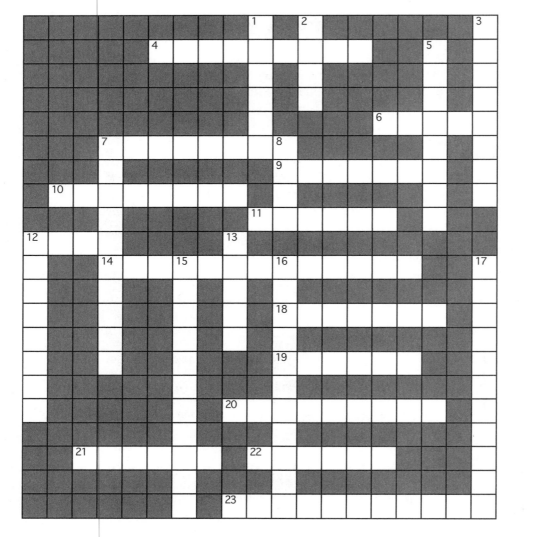

adverse
audible
coherent
competent
consecutive
consequence
data
defy
detain
dismal
inept
lament
parallel
perceptive
procrastinate
profound
seclusion
site
strategy
submit
summon
susceptible
transaction
valid
vocation

ACROSS

4. Capable; well qualified
6. Clumsy; unskillful
7. Deeply felt
9. Harmful; unfavorable
10. The same distance apart at every point
11. To express sorrow for or about; mourn for
12. The past, present or future location of a building or buildings or an event
14. To put off doing something until later
18. Able to be heard
19. To send for; order to come
20. The condition of being apart or far from others
21. To give in to another's authority or will; yield
22. Gloomy; cheerless; depressing
23. A result

DOWN

1. To delay; keep from continuing
2. To boldly oppose
3. A profession or occupation
5. Organized in a logical and orderly way
7. Understanding and insightful; observant; aware
8. Information gathered for a study or a decision
12. A method; overall plan
13. Firmly based on facts or logic; logical; based on good reasons
15. Following one after another without interruption
16. A business deal or action; exchange of money, goods, or services
17. Likely to be affected with or influenced; likely to be infected

UNIT FOUR: Test 1

PART A
Choose the word that best completes each item and write it in the space provided.

_____ 1. A huge mall now stands on the ___ where the racetrack had burned down.

    a. site   b. vocation   c. destiny   d. transaction

_____ 2. Bernard is ___ to headaches. Whenever he has to study, his head starts to pound.

    a. perceptive   b. susceptible   c. profound   d. parallel

_____ 3. The most important ___ in my parents' lives was the purchase of their house.

    a. destiny   b. severity   c. site   d. transaction

_____ 4. In ___ translation, words are translated as they are spoken. The translator has to be able to listen and talk at the same time.

    a. theoretical   b. simultaneous   c. morbid   d. obstinate

_____ 5. Tokyo, Japan, has a simple ___ for fitting as many people as possible onto rush-hour trains: workers are hired to push people on.

    a. seclusion   b. site   c. strategy   d. vocation

_____ 6. After doing a great deal of research, Sharon feels she now has enough ___ to begin writing her report on eating disorders.

    a. data   b. severity   c. seclusion   d. consequence

_____ 7. While Melba was pregnant, one of her students ___ German measles to her.

    a. confirmed   b. transmitted   c. detained   d. deteriorated

_____ 8. Instead of choosing a ___ typist, the supervisor hired someone who types with one finger and usually hits the wrong key.

    a. competent   b. theoretical   c. deceptive   d. conspicuous

_____ 9. My English instructor has such high standards that a B from her is ___ to an A from most other teachers.

    a. consecutive   b. adverse   c. comparable   d. innate

_____ 10. Doug bought orange socks instead of red because the store was poorly lit, and he couldn't ___ between the two colors.

    a. deteriorate   b. defy   c. dispense   d. discriminate

(Continues on next page)

PART B
On the answer line, write the letter of the choice that best completes each item.

_____ 11. Three **consecutive** months are
    a. January, March, May.
    c. July, June, April.
    b. August, September, October.
    d. January, June, July.

_____ 12. In order to **accelerate** a car, you must
    a. clean it thoroughly, inside and out.
    c. step on the gas pedal.
    b. take it to a service station.
    d. hit the brakes.

_____ 13. "It is my **destiny** to be a star," Melanie insisted. She obviously
    a. feared she'd never be a star.
    c. believed in fate.
    b. was interested in astronomy.
    d. has no talent.

_____ 14. During the **tedious** TV movie, I
    a. laughed until I actually fell off my chair.
    c. cried until I used up all my tissues.
    b. covered my face in horror.
    d. made a grocery list, just to pass the time.

_____ 15. "Enrique has **innate** talent for baseball," his coach said. "He
    a. is naturally clumsy."
    c. has never played the game."
    b. pitched well even in elementary school."
    d. has had to work harder than other players."

_____ 16. One product that is intended to **restrain** a person is
    a. handcuffs.
    c. a pair of sunglasses.
    b. an umbrella.
    d. a bicycle.

_____ 17. The two boys punched each other wildly, and then one **submitted** to the other, saying,
    a. "I'll beat you to a pulp!"
    c. "I give up."
    b. "Let's move this fight outside."
    d. "You're a yellow-bellied chicken!"

_____ 18. My dog's interest in the kitchen **diminished** when
    a. he realized the can I was opening was not for him.
    b. it was his usual lunchtime.
    c. someone in the kitchen called his name.
    d. he heard the sound of his dish being put on the floor.

_____ 19. Gina **lamented** her grade on the exam, saying,
    a. "I can't believe I did so well—I didn't even study!"
    b. "Naturally I got a good grade. I'm brilliant."
    c. "It's not great, but it's not awful either. It's what I deserved."
    d. "This is terrible! What am I going to do? Oh, I wish I had studied more."

_____ 20. After the little girl loudly announced, "I'm going to Japan tomorrow!" her mother **confirmed** her statement by saying,
    a. "You're *not* going to Japan. Where do you get these ideas?"
    b. "It's possible that we'll go to Japan next year, but nothing is certain."
    c. "No, honey. We're going to Jackson, not Japan."
    d. "That's right. My husband is in the military there, and we're going to join him."

Score (Number correct) _____ x 5 = _____ %

Enter your score above and in the vocabulary performance chart on the inside back cover of the book.

UNIT FOUR: Test 2

PART A
Complete each item with a word from the box. Use each word once.

a. **advocate**	b. **audible**	c. **deceptive**	d. **defy**	e. **deteriorate**
f. **dispense**	g. **intervene**	h. **parallel**	i. **perceptive**	j. **procrastinate**
k. **seclusion**	l. **summon**	m. **vocation**		

_____ 1. The prisoner was put in ___ after causing several fights with other inmates.

_____ 2. Certain servers at the school cafeteria ___ larger portions than others.

_____ 3. My aunt has trouble parking ___ to the curb. Her car is always farther out in back than in front.

_____ 4. My grandparents rarely ___ in family fights. They believe their children and grandchildren should work things out for themselves.

_____ 5. On Career Day, professionals came to the high school to tell students about their ___s.

_____ 6. No one responded when the speaker asked, "Can you hear me?" because his words were too soft to be ___.

_____ 7. I was shocked to see how my old school has ___(e)d since I moved away. It's in great need of repairs.

_____ 8. The picture in the magazine ad is ___. It makes the doll look much larger than it really is.

_____ 9. My counselor is very ___. The other day she knew something was bothering me even though I said, "I'm fine."

_____ 10. Vicky's children like to ___ her. No matter what she tells them to do, they'll do the opposite.

_____ 11. Jed ran to ___ the fire department when he saw smoke coming from his neighbor's window.

_____ 12. As a(n) ___ of public transportation, I try to convince more commuters to use buses and trains.

_____ 13. There's a club for people who like to ___. They haven't met yet because they keep postponing their first meeting.

(Continues on next page)

PART B

Write **C** if the italicized word is used **correctly**. Write **I** if the word is used **incorrectly**.

_____ 14. I felt much worse when my muscle cramp *subsided.*

_____ 15. When the nuclear power plant exploded, its dangers became *theoretical.*

_____ 16. We all thought the senator's speech was quite *coherent.* It was too disorganized to follow.

_____ 17. A camel's hump stores fat that breaks down into water. As a *consequence,* a camel can survive for as long as two weeks without drinking.

_____ 18. Joyce's baby is more *sedate* than most. When he isn't climbing all over the furniture, he's screaming.

_____ 19. Many Americans experienced *profound* depression after the terrorist attacks in New York City and Washington on September 11, 2001. They were greatly saddened by the deaths of thousands of innocent people.

_____ 20. When asked to pay for the window he had broken, Larry was *obstinate.* He said "Gladly," and paid for it immediately.

_____ 21. The owl can hardly move its eyes. So the ability to turn its head nearly completely around is *vital* to its survival.

_____ 22. I didn't realize the *severity* of Bill's injuries until I heard he was still in the hospital three months after his accident.

_____ 23. Koko is certainly *morbid.* The only movies she ever wants to see are musicals and light comedies.

_____ 24. I had to finish writing my report under *adverse* circumstances. It was late at night, the baby was crying, and my computer kept telling me it couldn't save what I had written.

_____ 25. Today, those who walk or drive in the city are *detained* by stoplights and traffic. In the future, however, moving sidewalks may make city travel faster by doing away with the need for vehicles and stoplights.

Score (Number correct) _____ x 4 = _____ %

Enter your score above and in the vocabulary performance chart on the inside back cover of the book.

UNIT FOUR: Test 3

PART A: Synonyms
PART A: Synonyms
In the space provided, write the letter of the choice that is most nearly the **same** in meaning as the **boldfaced** word.

_____ 1. **destiny**   **a)** delay   **b)** business deal   **c)** fate   **d)** hope

_____ 2. **obstinate**   **a)** discouraged   **b)** stubborn   **c)** calm   **d)** lively

_____ 3. **tedious**   **a)** inborn   **b)** neat   **c)** easy   **d)** boring

_____ 4. **parallel**   **a)** double   **b)** under   **c)** close   **d)** equally separated

_____ 5. **restrain**   **a)** hold back   **b)** learn again   **c)** compare   **d)** aid

_____ 6. **intervene**   **a)** give in   **b)** harm   **c)** come between   **d)** entertain

_____ 7. **site**   **a)** action   **b)** location   **c)** speed   **d)** occupation

_____ 8. **transaction**   **a)** information   **b)** travel   **c)** difficulty   **d)** business exchange

_____ 9. **consecutive**   **a)** official   **b)** likely to be affected by   **c)** deep   **d)** one after the other

_____ 10. **morbid**   **a)** horrifying   **b)** additional   **c)** satisfying   **d)** expensive

_____ 11. **dispense**   **a)** distinguish   **b)** give out   **c)** disobey   **d)** keep

_____ 12. **susceptible**   **a)** unclear   **b)** necessary   **c)** sensitive   **d)** understanding

_____ 13. **detain**   **a)** send   **b)** delay   **c)** cooperate   **d)** train

_____ 14. **data**   **a)** information   **b)** cause   **c)** method   **d)** conclusion

_____ 15. **severity**   **a)** large numbers   **b)** seriousness   **c)** stubbornness   **d)** celebration

_____ 16. **procrastinate**   **a)** admire   **b)** support   **c)** accomplish   **d)** put off

_____ 17. **discriminate**   **a)** break   **b)** worsen   **c)** assist   **d)** distinguish

_____ 18. **profound**   **a)** deep   **b)** lost   **c)** uninteresting   **d)** simple

_____ 19. **vital**   **a)** discouraging   **b)** inborn   **c)** important   **d)** unavoidable

_____ 20. **perceptive**   **a)** disgusting   **b)** insightful   **c)** unemotional   **d)** energetic

_____ 21. **simultaneous**   **a)** at the same time   **b)** in the same place   **c)** odd   **d)** unfavorable

_____ 22. **strategy**   **a)** battle   **b)** plan   **c)** officer   **d)** challenge

_____ 23. **seclusion**   **a)** barrier   **b)** job   **c)** apartness   **d)** boredom

_____ 24. **transmit**   **a)** pass along   **b)** give in   **c)** change   **d)** prevent

_____ 25. **summon**   **a)** release   **b)** arrest   **c)** add   **d)** send for

(Continues on next page)

PART B: Antonyms
In the space provided, write the letter of the choice that is most nearly the **opposite** in meaning to the **boldfaced** word.

_____ 26. **diminish**   a) increase   b) keep   c) know   d) forbid

_____ 27. **consequence**   a) explanation   b) membership   c) time   d) cause

_____ 28. **comparable**   a) free   b) different   c) available   d) known

_____ 29. **deteriorate**   a) improve   b) offer   c) worsen   d) claim

_____ 30. **competent**   a) late   b) angry   c) unskilled   d) calm

_____ 31. **accelerate**   a) plan   b) admit   c) require   d) slow down

_____ 32. **deceptive**   a) logical   b) truthful   c) skillful   d) lively

_____ 33. **coherent**   a) disconnected   b) boring   c) frightening   d) deep

_____ 34. **innate**   a) stiff   b) unclear   c) inborn   d) learned

_____ 35. **subside**   a) lean   b) increase   c) please   d) avoid

_____ 36. **defy**   a) lift   b) recognize   c) obey   d) look

_____ 37. **sedate**   a) hidden   b) tight   c) excited   d) sudden

_____ 38. **submit**   a) own   b) resist   c) forget   d) gather

_____ 39. **confirm**   a) deny   b) compete   c) win   d) clean up

_____ 40. **dismal**   a) unusual   b) cheerful   c) dull   d) modest

_____ 41. **vocation**   a) hobby   b) job   c) pay   d) barrier

_____ 42. **valid**   a) difficult   b) illogical   c) easy   d) long

_____ 43. **audible**   a) nearby   b) not able to be heard   c) able to be seen   d) logical

_____ 44. **adverse**   a) ready   b) colorful   c) favorable   d) well-known

_____ 45. **vigorous**   a) early   b) misleading   c) not alike   d) weak

_____ 46. **theoretical**   a) practical   b) simple   c) untrue   d) religious

_____ 47. **conspicuous**   a) illegal   b) calm   c) necessary   d) concealed

_____ 48. **inept**   a) unknown   b) guilty   c) skillful   d) clumsy

_____ 49. **advocate**   a) opponent   b) decision   c) follower   d) dishonest person

_____ 50. **lament**   a) forgive   b) regret   c) explain   d) rejoice

Score   (Number correct) _____ x 2 = _____ %

Enter your score above and in the vocabulary performance chart on the inside back cover of the book.

UNIT FOUR: Test 4

Each item below starts with a pair of words in CAPITAL LETTERS. For each item, figure out the relationship between these two words. Then decide which of the choices (*a*, *b*, *c*, or *d*) expresses a similar relationship. Write the letter of your choice on the answer line.

_____ 1. CONSEQUENCE : ACTION ::
  a. prediction : past   b. odor : sight
  c. effect : cause   d. absence: wish

_____ 2. DETAIN : DELAY ::
  a. hurry : slow down   b. dismiss : leave
  c. combine : separate   d. chat : talk

_____ 3. DIMINISH : INCREASE ::
  a. grow : mature   b. weaken : die
  c. fall : rise   d. spread : expand

_____ 4. VITAL : NECESSARY ::
  a. interesting : boring   b. useful : advice
  c. chosen : rejected   d. outstanding : superior

_____ 5. DISMAL : CHEERFUL ::
  a. old : antique   b. disappointing : satisfying
  c. relief : pain   d. real : actual

_____ 6. SUBSIDE : DECREASE ::
  a. spend : pay out   b. keep : discard
  c. look : avoid   d. run : walk

_____ 7. SUMMON : DISMISS ::
  a. drive : steer   b. try : struggle
  c. stay : remain   d. throw : catch

_____ 8. VOCATION : TEACHING ::
  a. work : vacation   b. hobby : gardening
  c. salary : bill   d. strength : weakness

_____ 9. INEPT : SKILLFUL ::
  a. cautious : careful   b. glad : rewarding
  c. lovely : colorful   d. sweet : sour

_____ 10. OBSTINATE : MULE ::
  a. vicious : lamb   b. loyal : dog
  c. tiny : whale   d. safe : wolf

(Continues on next page)

_____ 11. PERCEPTIVE : OBSERVE ::

    a. happy : mourn   b. emotional : feel
    c. sad : rejoice   d. forgetful : remember

_____ 12. DATA : TEST SCORES ::

    a. carrots : peas   b. music : paintings
    c. books : novels   d. numbers : letters

_____ 13. DEFY : OBEY ::

    a. fight : win   b. enlarge : shrink
    c. defend : fight   d. insist : demand

_____ 14. SECLUSION : SOLITARY CONFINEMENT ::

    a. school : library   b. relaxation : court
    c. cold : freezer   d. light source : candle

_____ 15. VALID : UNTRUE ::

    a. waterproofed : rainy   b. proved : factual
    c. insulated : protected   d. confusing : clear

_____ 16. VIGOROUS : JOGGING ::

    a. relaxed : boxing   b. peaceful: meditating
    c. unkind : praying   d. ancient : jumping rope

_____ 17. CONSPICUOUS : SEE ::

    a. touch : feel   b. perfume: smell
    c. loud : hear   d. tongue : taste

_____ 18. ADVERSE : UNFAVORABLE ::

    a. good : luck   b. average : ordinary
    c. bad : worse   d. ugly : attractive

_____ 19. ADVOCATE : SUPPORTS ::

    a. assistant : helps   b. enemy : loses
    c. manager : waits   d. king : obeys

_____ 20. COHERENT : ILLOGICAL ::

    a. organized : orderly   b. forceful : weak
    c. long : lengthy   d. clear : reasoned

Score   (Number correct) _____ x 5 = _____ %

Enter your score above and in the vocabulary performance chart on the inside back cover of the book.

Appendixes

A. Limited Answer Key

Important Note: Be sure to use this answer key as a learning tool only. You should not turn to this key until you have considered carefully the sentence in which a given word appears.

Used properly, the key will help you to learn words and to prepare for the activities and tests for which answers are not given. For ease of reference, the title of the "Final Check" passage in each chapter appears in parentheses.

Chapter 1 (Taking Exams)

Sentence Check 1

1. candid
2. anecdote
3. drastic
4. avert
5. concise
6. comply
7. compel
8. alternative
9. acknowledge
10. appropriate

Chapter 2 (Nate the Woodsman)

Sentence Check 1

1. erratic
2. refuge
3. fortify
4. forfeit
5. isolate
6. reminisce
7. illuminate
8. dialog
9. extensive
10. urban

Chapter 3 (Who's on Trial?)

Sentence Check 1

1. impartial
2. undermine
3. menace
4. morale
5. legitimate
6. naive
7. delete
8. overt
9. lenient
10. integrity

Chapter 4 (Night Nurse)

Sentence Check 1

1. gruesome
2. erode
3. imply
4. novice
5. idealistic
6. hypocrite
7. endorse
8. impact
9. obstacle
10. illusion

Chapter 5 (Relating to Parents)

Sentence Check 1

1. scapegoat
2. sustain
3. denounce
4. concede
5. deter
6. superficial
7. disclose
8. transition
9. contrary
10. conservative

Chapter 6 (Job Choices)

Sentence Check 1

1. derive
2. verify
3. moderate
4. tentative
5. surpass
6. supplement
7. inhibit
8. conceive
9. diversity
10. compensate

Chapter 7 (Museum Pet)

Sentence Check 1

1. phobia
2. anonymous
3. acute
4. arrogant
5. recipient
6. bestow
7. prudent
8. apprehensive
9. donor
10. prominent

Chapter 8 (Our Headstrong Baby)

Sentence Check 1

1. prevail
2. propel
3. retrieve
4. exempt
5. accessible
6. awe
7. compatible
8. cite
9. rational
10. retort

Chapter 9 (A Narrow Escape)

Sentence Check 1

1. fluent
2. harass
3. obsession
4. evasive
5. elapse
6. lethal
7. ordeal
8. futile
9. persistent
10. infer

Chapter 10 (The Power of Advertising)

Sentence Check 1

1. devise
2. universal
3. savor
4. subtle
5. vivid
6. stimulate
7. convey
8. delusion
9. unique
10. versatile

Chapter 11 (Waiter)

Sentence Check 1

1. inevitable
2. option
3. equate
4. passive
5. patron
6. malicious
7. impose
8. indignant
9. defer
10. endeavor

Chapter 12 (Adjusting to a New Culture)

Sentence Check 1

1. dismay
2. recede
3. refute
4. gesture
5. retain
6. revert
7. adapt
8. exile
9. reciprocate
10. ritual

Chapter 13 (A Dream About Wealth)

Sentence Check 1

1. mediocre
2. indulgent
3. emerge
4. notable
5. liberal
6. elaborate
7. indifferent
8. frugal
9. impulsive
10. exotic

Chapter 14 (Children and Drugs)

Sentence Check 1

1. coerce
2. sadistic
3. impair
4. essence
5. immunity
6. affirm
7. alleged
8. elite
9. query
10. allude

Chapter 15 (Party House)

Sentence Check 1

1. ridicule
2. stereotype
3. plausible
4. shrewd
5. recur
6. tactic
7. skeptical
8. reprimand
9. provoke
10. revoke

Chapter 16 (Procrastinator)

Sentence Check 1

1. transaction
2. diminish
3. procrastinate
4. consequence
5. simultaneous
6. strategy
7. destiny
8. vital
9. detain
10. tedious

Chapter 17 (A Change in View)

Sentence Check 1

1. discriminate
2. profound
3. subside
4. summon
5. vocation
6. dismal
7. dispense
8. severity
9. theoretical
10. site

Chapter 18 (Family Differences)

Sentence Check 1

1. data
2. inept
3. morbid
4. sedate
5. parallel
6. perceptive
7. intervene
8. obstinate
9. lament
10. innate

Chapter 19 (Chicken Pox)

Sentence Check 1

1. vigorous
2. valid
3. susceptible
4. confirm
5. submit
6. seclusion
7. restrain
8. deceptive
9. transmit
10. defy

Chapter 20 (Walking)

Sentence Check 1

1. conspicuous
2. competent
3. adverse
4. advocate
5. accelerate
6. audible
7. deteriorate
8. comparable
9. coherent
10. consecutive

B. Dictionary Use

It isn't always possible to figure out the meaning of a word from its context, and that's where a dictionary comes in. Following is some basic information to help you use a dictionary.

HOW TO FIND A WORD

A dictionary contains so many words that it can take a while to find the one you're looking for. But if you know how to use guide words, you can find a word rather quickly. *Guide words* are the two words at the top of each dictionary page. The first guide word tells what the first word is on the page. The second guide word tells what the last word is on that page. The other words on a page fall alphabetically between the two guide words. So when you look up a word, find the two guide words that alphabetically surround the word you're looking for.

• Which of the following pair of guide words would be on a page with the word *skirmish*?

   skimp / skyscraper   skyward / slave   sixty / skimming

The answer to this question and the questions that follow are given on the next page.

HOW TO USE A DICTIONARY LISTING

A dictionary listing includes many pieces of information. For example, here is a typical listing. Note that it includes much more than just a definition.

> **driz•zle** (drĭz′əl) *v.* **-zled, -zling.** To rain gently and steadily in fine drops.
> — *n.* A very light rain. —**driz′zly,** *adj.*

Key parts of a dictionary entry are listed and explained below.

Syllables. Dots separate dictionary entry words into syllables. Note that *drizzle* has one dot, which breaks the word into two syllables.

• To practice seeing the syllable breakdown in a dictionary entry, write the number of syllables in each word below.

   glam•our _____   **mi•cro•wave** _____   **in•de•scrib•a•ble** _____

Pronunciation guide. The information within parentheses after the entry word shows how to pronounce the entry word. This pronunciation guide includes two types of symbols: pronunciation symbols and accent marks.

Pronunciation symbols represent the consonant sounds and vowel sounds in a word. The consonant sounds are probably very familiar to you, but you may find it helpful to review some of the sounds of the vowels—*a, e, i, o,* and *u.* Every dictionary has a key explaining the sounds of its pronunciation symbols, including the long and short sounds of vowels.

Long vowels have the sound of their own names. For example, the *a* in *pay* and the *o* in *no* both have long vowel sounds. Long vowel sounds are shown by a straight line above the vowel.

In many dictionaries, the *short vowels* are shown by a curved line above the vowel. Thus the *i* in the first syllable of *drizzle* is a short *i.* The pronunciation chart on the inside front cover of this book indicates that the short *i* has the sound of *i* in *sit.* It also indicates that the short *a* has the sound of *a* in *hat,* that the short *e* has the sound of *e* in *ten,* and so on.

• Which of the words below have a short vowel sound? Which has a long vowel sound?

   drug _____   **night** _____   **sand** _____

Another pronunciation symbol is the *schwa* (ə), which looks like an upside-down e. It stands for certain rapidly spoken, unaccented vowel sounds, such as the *a* in *above*, the *e* in *item*, the *i* in *easily*, the *o* in *gallop*, and the *u* in *circus*. More generally, it has an "uh" sound, like the "uh" a speaker makes when hesitating. Here are three words that include the schwa sound:

in•fant (ĭn′fənt)   **bum•ble** (bŭm′bəl)   **de•liv•er** (dĭ-lĭv′ər)

• Which syllable in *drizzle* contains the schwa sound, the first or the second? _____

Accent marks are small black marks that tell you which syllable to emphasize, or stress, as you say a word. An accent mark follows *driz* in the pronunciation guide for *drizzle,* which tells you to stress the first syllable of *drizzle*. Syllables with no accent mark are not stressed. Some syllables are in between, and they are marked with a lighter accent mark.

• Which syllable has the stronger accent in *sentimental*? _____

sen•ti•men•tal (sĕn′tə-mĕn′tl)

Parts of speech. After the pronunciation key and before each set of definitions, the entry word's parts of speech are given. The parts of speech are abbreviated as follows:

noun—*n.*   pronoun—*pron.*   adjective—*adj.*   adverb—*adv.*   verb—*v.*

• The listing for *drizzle* shows that it can be two parts of speech. Write them below:

_____   _____

Definitions. Words often have more than one meaning. When they do, each meaning is usually numbered in the dictionary. You can tell which definition of a word fits a given sentence by the meaning of the sentence. For example, the word *charge* has several definitions, including these two: **1.** To ask as a price. **2.** To accuse or blame.

• Show with a check which definition (1 or 2) applies in each sentence below:

The store charged me less for the blouse because it was missing a button.   1 ___   2 ___

My neighbor has been charged with shoplifting.   1 ___   2 ___

Other information. After the definitions in a listing in a hardbound dictionary, you may get information about the *origin* of a word. Such information about origins, also known as *etymology,* is usually given in brackets. And you may sometimes be given one or more synonyms or antonyms for the entry word. *Synonyms* are words that are similar in meaning to the entry word; *antonyms* are words that are opposite in meaning.

WHICH DICTIONARIES TO OWN

You will find it useful to own two recent dictionaries: a small paperback dictionary to carry to class and a hardbound dictionary, which contains more information than a small paperback version. Among the good dictionaries strongly recommended are both the paperback and the hardcover editions of the following:

The American Heritage Dictionary
The Random House College Dictionary
Webster's New World Dictionary

ANSWERS TO THE DICTIONARY QUESTIONS
Guide words: *skimp/skyscraper*
Number of syllables: 2, 3, 5
Vowels: *drug, sand* (short); *night* (long)
Schwa: second syllable of *drizzle*

Accent: stronger accent on third syllable *(men)*
Parts of speech: noun and verb
Definitions: 1; 2

C. Topics for Discussion and Writing

Note: The first three items for each chapter are intended for discussion; the last three, for writing. Feel free, however, to either talk or write about any of the items.

Chapter 1 (Taking Exams)

1. Just about everyone catches a cold or the flu from time to time, but there are ways to lessen one's chances of infection. What are some methods you would recommend to **avert** sickness?

2. What is considered **appropriate** dress at your school or workplace? Do you think people in a school or an office should be **compelled** to dress a certain way? Why or why not?

3. When someone says, "Tell me the truth," should you always **comply**? Is there such a thing as being too **candid**?

4. Imagine that your class has been asked to produce a collection of short, true stories. Write out a favorite family **anecdote** that would be suitable to include in such a collection.

5. What are you hoping to do after you complete your education? Write about several **alternatives** you might pursue.

6. Think of someone you know who has made a truly **drastic** change in his or her life. Write a paper about that person's life change and its results.

Chapter 2 (Nate the Woodsman)

1. Where would you prefer to live: in the country, or in a more **urban** setting? Why? If you had to forever **forfeit** any chance of living in the other setting, is there anything you would miss?

2. Think of someone who has an **extensive** collection—for example, of baseball cards, Barbie dolls, or travel souvenirs. Why might this person enjoy collecting? If you're a collector yourself, tell about your own reasons for the hobby.

3. When you know you have a demanding day ahead, what do you do to **fortify** yourself?

4. Do you know someone—a grandparent, perhaps, or an older friend—who likes to **reminisce** about his or her younger days? Write a paper describing some of this person's memories. You might begin with a topic sentence such as this: *When my grandmother lived with my family, she told me many rich stories about her childhood.*

5. Almost everyone has times that he or she wants to be alone. When you want to **isolate** yourself, where do you go? Describe this special place in writing. When you take **refuge** in this place, what do you like to do or think about?

6. Have you ever had a teacher, employer, or acquaintance whose **erratic** behavior made him or her hard to deal with? Write a paper in which you describe the person's actions and your response to them.

Chapter 3 (Who's on Trial?)

1. What do you think are the worst **menaces** threatening the environment? Explain what you feel the dangers are and any ideas you have on how to deal with them.

2. Would you say your parents were **lenient** with you—or were they strict? Were they **impartial** with their children, or did they seem to prefer one child or another? Give examples.

3. If you were a teacher, what would you consider **legitimate** excuses for students' not having homework done? What excuses, if any, would you *not* accept?

4. Write a paper about someone in public life or someone you know who has **integrity**. What has this person done or said to make you think he or she is especially moral?

5. If you could undo the past, what is one experience in your life you would **delete**? Write a paper in which you explain this occurrence and why you'd like to erase it from your life.

6. Have you ever been the victim of **overt** prejudice because of your race, sex, or another characteristic? Describe the incident. How did it leave you feeling? Did it **undermine** your **morale**, or did it have another effect? If you prefer, write about another person's experience with prejudice.

Chapter 4 (Night Nurse)

1. With your classmates, brainstorm a list of celebrities you've seen **endorse** products on television. Does a celebrity's support make you think a product is a good one? Why or why not?

2. What are some of the most **gruesome** movies you've ever seen? What made them gruesome? How do you respond to such films?

3. Think of something that you would like very much to have or to achieve. What is the biggest **obstacle** that stands between you and this goal? How might you remove this obstacle?

4. Which word better describes you: *idealistic* or *practical*? Write a paper in which you explain why you chose the word you did, giving examples to prove your point.

5. Write a paper in which you describe a time a person you know acted as a **hypocrite**. In your mind, what did the person's actions **imply** about his or her character? Here's a sample topic sentence for this paper: *When I learned that an "old friend" of mine was a hypocrite, I realized his/her character was very different from what I had supposed.*

6. Probably everyone has believed something was true, but later realized it was just an **illusion**. For instance, you might have felt someone was angry at you, and later discovered he or she was angry about something else. Write a paper about a time you were mistaken about something. Did discovering you were wrong **erode** your self-confidence, or did you feel it had been an understandable mistake?

Chapter 5 (Relating to Parents)

1. Suppose you've been told an important secret. Under what circumstances might it be better to **disclose** this information? Why?

2. Do you believe that capital punishment **deters** people from committing murder? If not, do you think execution serves any purpose?

3. In your opinion, which television programs present more than a **superficial** view of their subject? What important themes do these programs deal with? Give examples.

4. Have you ever felt that you've been unfairly used as a **scapegoat** in some situation? How did you respond? Did you **denounce** the person who tried to blame you? Write about the situation and its outcome.

5. Think of two people you know with **contrary** personalities: one quite **conservative**, resisting change and liking to do things the tried-and-true way, and the other more adventurous, always wanting to try something new. Write a paper that contrasts these two people and their very different approaches to life.

6. Life is typically full of changes—from being a high-school student to being a college student, from being single to being part of a couple (or vice versa), and so on. Write a paper describing a **transition** in your own life that was difficult. How did you **sustain** your good humor and belief in yourself during this time of change?

Chapter 6 (Job Choices)

1. Many people have hobbies from which they **derive** enjoyment and satisfaction. Do you have a hobby? What is it? How much **diversity** in hobbies is there among your classmates?

2. Do you know someone who "moonlights" at a second job in order to **supplement** his or her income? What sacrifices has the person made in order to hold two jobs at once? In your opinion, do the benefits of the second job outweigh the drawbacks? Why or why not?

3. What do you expect to do next summer? Are your plans **tentative**, or are they definite?

4. Suppose you were in charge of coming up with ideas to **inhibit** people from drinking and driving in your community. What can you **conceive** of that might be effective? Write a paper explaining your ideas.

5. Think of something you've tried to accomplish recently, but with which you have had only **moderate** success. Maybe you've tried to eat healthier foods, improve your grades, or get along better with someone. Write a paper about what you tried to do, how well or poorly it worked, and if you plan to **surpass** these efforts in the future.

6. People choose careers for different reasons, such as personal satisfaction, how the job **compensates** them financially, and the ability to use their talents. Write a paper about your career plans and why a certain career appeals to you.

Chapter 7 (Museum Pet)

1. Certain situations make almost everyone **apprehensive**. For example, many people get nervous about taking tests, speaking in public, and going on job interviews. What are a few situations that make you apprehensive? A **phobia**, on the other hand, is far more extreme than a normal feeling of apprehension. Does anyone you know suffer from a phobia? What is the person so afraid of? What does the phobia keep him or her from doing?

2. Some newspapers will publish **anonymous** letters to the editor. Others refuse to print letters unless the writer's name is signed. Which policy do you think is better? Why? Are there good reasons that a writer might not want his or her name attached to a letter?

3. Every neighborhood has some features—maybe a particular store, tree, or house—that stand out for some reason. What are some **prominent** sights in your neighborhood? What makes them prominent?

4. A person who applies for a driver's license may sign a card stating that upon death, he or she will allow his or her organs—such as the heart, lungs, or kidneys—to be given to someone who needs them. Would you be an organ **donor**? Write a paper in which you explain why or why not.

5. Imagine that you have a child. (If you do have a child, think of him or her.) If you were able to **bestow** one quality upon that child, what would it be? Courage? The ability to love others? Kindness? Intelligence? Good business sense? Write a paper explaining which single quality you would give the child and why.

6. Write a paper describing a time when you acted in a way that was not **prudent**. What did you do? What happened as a result? Did you learn anything useful from the experience?

Chapter 8 (Our Headstrong Baby)

1. Who is a person—living or dead—for whom you would feel real **awe** if the two of you could meet? Why do you regard this person with such great respect?

2. What are two foods you like to eat together, or two articles of clothing you like to wear together, that most people would not think are **compatible**? What do you like about this combination?

3. Do you think that people who object to serving in the military for religious reasons should be **exempt** from military service? Why or why not?

4. Some people get married after giving the decision a lot of **rational** thought. Others plunge into marriage largely on the basis of their emotions. Write about which style of decision-making you think leads to better marriages. **Cite** examples to back up your opinion.

5. Write a paper about a recent argument you've had with someone close to you. What was the argument about? In the end, whose opinion do you think **prevailed**?

6. How do you deal with unwanted telephone sales calls? Do you talk to the caller politely? Hang up? Make a rude **retort**? Write about how you respond to such calls—and why.

Chapter 9 (A Narrow Escape)

1. Many people feel that **lethal** weapons are too easily available in our society. Do you agree? What controls, if any, do you think there should be on gun sales and ownership?

2. What examples have you heard of that show a fan's unhealthy **obsession** with a celebrity? In your opinion, would the rewards of being famous make up for the possibility of going through such an **ordeal**?

3. Take a survey in your class: How many students are **fluent** in two languages? Three? More than three? How many have relatives who are fluent in two or more languages? Has the knowledge of additional languages affected people's lives in any way?

4. Sometimes when a guy or girl asks someone out, the other person gives an **evasive** answer such as "Not this weekend" or "I'll think about it." Write a paper about the effect of such an answer. Does it make the one who asks more **persistent**, thinking he or she will hear "yes" another time? Or would he or she conclude it's **futile** to ask again?

5. In most schools there are bullies and people they make a habit of picking on. Write a paper about a bully you've observed and the person (or people) the bully **harassed**. What can you **infer** about why the bully acted the way he or she did?

6. What do you do in the time that **elapses** between the minute you get home after school or work and the time you go to bed? Write a paper that describes a typical evening for you.

Chapter 10 (The Power of Advertising)

1. If you were in charge of decorating a restaurant, what colors would you use? Do you think that **vivid** colors **stimulate** the appetite, or do soft, pastel colors make people hungrier? In other words, what kind of surroundings make you really **savor** your food?

2. As you were growing up, did your parents have certain "looks" or signals that **conveyed** unspoken messages to you—such as "Stop that!" or "We're leaving now"? What were some of your family's **unique** messages that were communicated without words?

3. Little children often develop some innocent **delusions**: for instance, some assume that their teachers live at their school. Can you remember having any such mistaken beliefs? Or does a child you know have such a belief?

4. If you saw a picture of yourself taken a few years ago next to a picture of yourself taken today, what differences would you notice? Write a paper describing those differences, indicating whether they are **subtle** or dramatic.

5. Some countries have a policy of **universal** military service: Every person, male and female, spends several years in the country's army. Would you support such a policy in this country? Write a paper explaining why or why not.

6. Imagine that you are a very creative inventor—maybe even a bit of a mad scientist. Write a humorous paper describing "The Household Friend," a marvelous machine that you have **devised**. This **versatile** machine can do a number of helpful tasks around the house. A reading machine, for instance, might provide light for reading, play soft background music, and turn a page at your command. Include details of your machine's appearance and functions.

Chapter 11 (Waiter)

1. How do people in your family behave during an argument? Are any of them **passive** people who sit back, say little, and let others do the talking? Do any tend to be **malicious**, making hurtful remarks? And what is *your* argument style? Give examples.

2. Describe a store or restaurant where you are a regular **patron**. Do you visit that place often because you have no other **option**, or is there something about it that you particularly like? If so, what is it?

3. People become **indignant** when they or someone else is **imposed** upon or otherwise treated unfairly. Describe an occasion when you were angry because a person was unfair to you or someone else. What did you do or say in response?

4. Have you **endeavored** to warn a friend that something he or she was doing would get him or her in trouble, but the friend ignored your warning? How did you feel when the **inevitable** result occurred, and the friend *did* get in trouble? How did the friend respond? Write a paper describing what happened.

5. An old line from the cartoon "Peanuts" is "Happiness is a warm puppy." What quality or thing do you **equate** with happiness? Write a paper in which you complete and explain this sentence: "For me, happiness is _____."

6. Have you ever **deferred** to someone in an argument, even though you really believed that you were right? Why did you give in? Do you think now that giving in was the best thing to do? Write a paper describing the argument, what you did, and how you now feel about it.

Chapter 12 (Adjusting to a New Culture)

1. Athletes are well-known for having certain **rituals**. For instance, a baseball pitcher may go through a series of "good-luck" motions before he throws the ball. Share with your classmates any good-luck ritual you may have for a specific situation, such as playing a sport or taking a test. When did you begin using this ritual, and why?

2. Think of a time when you began something new, such as going to a new school, starting a new job, or moving to a new home or city. What were some of the things that **dismayed** you at first about the new experience? Did you eventually **adapt** to those things, or do they still bother you?

3. When someone gives you a compliment or does you a favor, do you always feel you must **reciprocate**? What **gestures** have you used to show how you feel about someone in one of those situations?

4. When something bad happens to you, what helps you to **retain** your good spirits and a positive attitude? Talking with friends? Applying your sense of humor? Exercising? Explain in writing how you try to overcome the effects of an unhappy circumstance.

5. Have you ever stopped a bad habit and then **reverted** to it? Write a paper explaining what the habit was, how long you were able to avoid it, and why you began it again.

6. Do you think this country should have the death penalty? Do you think cigarette smoking should be outlawed? Write a paper explaining your reasoning on *one* of those two questions. Also **refute** some of the reasons someone arguing on the other side might offer.

Chapter 13 (A Dream About Wealth)

1. What is one **exotic** place you've never been to, but would like to visit? Why would you like to go there? Share with your classmates what you know about this place and why it appeals to you.

2. You'd love to go out and have some fun this weekend, but your supply of money has nearly run out. Brainstorm with your class ways to amuse yourself while still being **frugal**.

3. What are some problems facing your school that you think people are **indifferent** to? Examine ways each problem might be solved. Perhaps some practical solutions will **emerge** from your discussion.

4. Think of an activity that requires **elaborate** preparation—otherwise the results will be, at best, **mediocre**. Possibilities include a surprise party, a school paper, or a satisfying meal. Make a list of everything you need to do ahead of time. Then write a paper of advice on how to make the project a success.

5. Write a paper about someone you know who is **impulsive**. In your paper, include an interesting example of a time that this person acted without thinking ahead.

6. What do you think of **indulgent** parents who give **liberal** presents and privileges to their children, no matter how the children behave? Write a paper explaining why that style of parenting has either good or bad results. Include specific examples, such as what happens when parents do children's chores for them or when children are allowed to come home as late as they wish.

Chapter 14 (Children and Drugs)

1. Sadly, there are incidents involving children who are **alleged** to have committed serious offenses, such as the six-year-old boy who picked up a loaded gun and shot his sister. In your opinion, should young children be tried in court for these offenses, or should their age give them **immunity** from criminal charges?

2. Suppose you have been admitted to an **elite** group: those reporters whose job it is to question the President of the United States. At the next presidential press conference, you will be permitted to **query** the President on any topic you wish. What question would you ask, and why?

3. Some people think products that **impair** our health, such as cigarettes and alcoholic beverages, should be made illegal. Do you agree? Or do you feel that it's wrong to pass laws that **coerce** people to do what's good for them?

4. Imagine that you'd like to make a friend aware of a bad habit and how much it annoys others, but you don't want to say anything too obvious. How might you **allude** to the habit and how to deal with it? Write a paper in which you describe your friend's habit and explain how and what you would hint to him or her about it.

5. We may not always **affirm** our feelings for others in words, but we can show our feelings in other ways. We might, for instance, do a chore for a grandparent or help a friend paint a bedroom. Write about how your family and/or friends have affirmed feelings for one another through both speech and actions.

6. We all have different heroes, but our heroes probably have a good deal in common. What would you say is the **essence** of heroism? Write a paper beginning with the topic sentence *The essence of heroism is* _____. Then develop your paper with at least one example of someone whose character or actions demonstrate this quality.

Chapter 15 (Party House)

1. You were supposed to give an oral report in class today, but you forgot to prepare it. You don't want to make up a report because you think you'd look like a fool and your classmates might **ridicule** you. What **plausible** excuse could you give for your lack of preparation? Brainstorm a list of such excuses with your classmates.

2. In your opinion, what are some of the best **tactics** for doing well on a test? See how long a list of suggestions you and your classmates can create.

3. What are some of the ways that young children **provoke** their older brothers and sisters or their parents? Why is this behavior so annoying? What can older children or parents do to make sure that it will not **recur** in the future?

4. Have you or has someone you know ever had a privilege **revoked**? In a paper, describe the situation that resulted in losing the privilege. How long did it take to earn it back again?

5. Write about an incident that taught you how wrong a **stereotype** can be. For example, you might have met an older person with very "young" ideas or behavior. Begin with a topic sentence like this: *Before I met _____, I believed the stereotype that all _____s were _____, but I know better now.*

6. You are the manager of a store in which a new employee has made a habit of leaving twenty minutes early, with excuses such as needing to take a relative to the doctor or to meet a friend for dinner. The store owner asks you to write a **reprimand** to this employee, telling him what he has done wrong and making suggestions for future behavior. What would you say? Write the full reprimand you would give the employee.

Chapter 16 (Procrastinator)

1. Do you believe your future is largely determined by **destiny**, by pure luck, or by your own actions? Explain your point of view.

2. What might your closest friend worry about? Rather than simply saying, "Forget about it," what could you do to **diminish** his or her anxiety?

3. Imagine that you have made **simultaneous** commitments to meet two different people. One is an older relative who is depending on your help. The other is someone your own age who would be a great deal more fun to spend time with. Which commitment do you honor? Why?

4. When was the last time you **procrastinated**? What did you delay doing, and what were the **consequences**? Describe the situation in a paper, using either a humorous or a serious approach.

5. Think of an activity you regard as **tedious**—for example, waiting in line at a supermarket or doing a really boring household chore. What **strategy** do you use to make the activity more bearable? Write a paper of advice on how to pass the time during boring activities.

6. Most of us have things we think we cannot do without—in addition to the obvious ones: food, water, clothing, shelter. Besides these, what things—either major or minor—would you say are **vital** to you at this point in your life? Describe at least three of them in a paper and explain why they are so important to you.

Chapter 17 (A Change in View)

1. Suppose two young men are found guilty of robbing a convenience store. The first is a well-to-do college student who committed the robbery on a dare. The second man is out of work and needed money to buy food and medicine for a sick child. Should the two men receive different sentences? Or should the **severity** of the punishment be the same for both?

2. Think of the last time you were really angry with someone. What did you do to make your anger **subside**?

3. Many people read and write to newspaper advice columns for help with serious questions, such as what to do about a disturbed child or how to handle a **profound** loss. In your opinion, should advice columnists have to take courses in psychology and human relations—even pass exams and obtain degrees—before they are permitted to give advice on such matters? Why or why not?

4. If you were about to complete your education and go to work, what would your dream career be like? Write a paper about your ideal **vocation**.

5. Make a list of several **sites** in your community that are **dismal**. Use this list to write a paper on how to make your community more cheerful and inviting by improving those places.

6. Imagine this problem: The same required course is taught by two different teachers. Students may sign up for whichever teacher they prefer. How could a student **discriminate** between the two teachers? Offer some suggestions in a paper.

Chapter 18 (Family Differences)

1. A common belief is that men are **inept** when it comes to observing others' feelings and expressing their own, while women are emotionally **perceptive** and communicative. Do you agree? Use examples from your own experience to either support or attack these views.

2. Do you feel it is harmful for young children to watch **morbid** scenes—for example, of brutal attacks and murders—in the movies and on television? If you've known of children who have watched such scenes, how do you think the experiences affected them?

3. Older people sometimes **lament** the loss of a simpler society, saying sadly that life is more complicated or dangerous now than it was years ago. What recent changes in society do you think are for the worse? Which do you think are valuable? Consider, for example, the influence of home computers or sport utility vehicles.

4. Which of your abilities would you identify as purely **innate**? Write a paper describing one or more talents of yours and how you have or have not developed them.

5. How do you usually respond to a crisis? Do you remain **sedate**, or do you become so disturbed that someone must **intervene** to calm you down? Write a paper about your response to crises. Provide one or two examples.

6. Imagine you've decided it's time to move somewhere completely new, but you're unsure about where. What kinds of **data** would you need to help you make the decision about where to go? Which specific qualities of a city would you be **obstinate** about? Which would you be more flexible about?

Chapter 19 (Chicken Pox)

1. As you must know, being a student can be stressful. Brainstorm with classmates some steps students can take to make themselves less **susceptible** to school-related stress.

2. Many criticize TV and magazine advertisements for being **deceptive**. Describe and discuss some examples of ads you feel are misleading. What is misleading about them?

3. Share with classmates your ideal vacation. Do you seek relaxation and **seclusion**—or **vigorous** sports and excitement? What are some places you think would fit your vacation ideal? Do your classmates have similar or very different visions of the ideal vacation?

4. We have all been in situations where we tried to **restrain** ourselves from doing something that was not appropriate. Maybe we had to hold back giggles in class or found ourselves staring impolitely at someone. Write a paper describing in detail a time you had difficulty keeping yourself from acting improperly.

5. Have you ever discovered that a juicy rumor about someone (even yourself) was not **valid** and people were passing it around without **confirming** it? Write a paper telling what the rumor was, how it spread, and what you think the truth of the matter was.

6. Describe a time when you **defied** a rule that you now feel you should have **submitted** to. For instance, you might have skipped many days of school when you were younger and now realize you harmed your education. Write about one or more such times, explaining why you regret not following the rule(s).

Chapter 20 (Walking)

1. What are some **adverse** conditions in your school? Overcrowded classes? A building that's beginning to **deteriorate**? A lack of school spirit? Brainstorm with classmates a list of school problems as well as some ways that they might be overcome.

2. Tell about someone you know who is especially **competent** at what he or she does. After classmates have described their choices, try to identify together the qualities and habits that are shared by all these skillful people.

3. How are playing the piano and riding a bike alike? The answer is that you may become rusty, but you never forget how to do them. Name two other activities that, on the surface, are very dissimilar but on closer examination are actually **comparable** in some way. For instance, how are cooking and eating alike?

4. Two keys to a successful classroom presentation are being **audible** and **coherent**. What are some others? Prepare a short list of ingredients for a successful speech. Then use the list to write a paper in which you explain how to go about "wowing" your classmates and instructor with a presentation.

5. An old saying goes, "When it rains, it pours." Think of a time in your life when two or more **consecutive** bad events—or good events—happened. Write a paper describing the negative or positive occurrences, their effects on you, and your reactions.

6. Think of a position of which you are a firm **advocate**. Are you a strong supporter of recycling? Of teaching a second language to elementary-school students? Write a paper in which you try to persuade the reader of the correctness of your position. Begin by stating your position in your topic sentence: *Every elementary-school student should be taught a second language.* Then go on to present and explain one or more reasons—for example: *First of all, contact with people in other countries, either in person or on the Internet, is becoming more common. . . .*

D. Word List

Notes

Notes

Notes

Notes

Notes

Smcquee16760